Circles In The Sand

Alastair Walker

Copyright © 2015 Alastair Walker

All rights reserved.

ISBN-13:978-1517620660

DEDICATION

For my Dad, who bought me my first motorcycle.

ACKNOWLEDGMENTS

Thanks to Carole Nash Insurance and BMW Motorrad GB who helped make the trip possible.

No thanks to the manufacturers of Lariam, who made another kind of trip possible

FOREWORD

This is the story of the toughest, maddest, longest motorcycle, car and truck race in the world. It's the Everest of enduro; a skin-cracking adventure across a parched river of sand. People have died on this rally; racers, crew, journalists, pilots - it is, as one journalist said years ago, 'like war without the bullets.'

The Paris-Dakar is a different thing now. They run it in South America, where there is less chance of terrorist attack, although it remains a test of speed, organisation, skill, endurance and cold hard cash. Yes, cash always helps, especially in Africa, which is a beautiful, corrupt, dangerous and soul-changing continent.

Back in 2001, I finally got the chance to fulfil a lifelong dream; to cover the Paris-Dakar as a journalist, to see it from the inside as a raw, unedited slice of brutal competition. Flashes of life blazing over an empty quarter of this Earth.

In the space of a month, I learned to sleep on a runway, even when jet turbines whistled about 200 metres away. I grew face fuzz, felt my brain boiling in the Sahara heat and became part werewolf, watching the moon and satellites slow-dance over the Atlas Mountains as Lariam drove me slowly crazy with its hallucinations.

I wantonly drank beer and ate too much, whilst starving faces pressed against the fences around our compound and saw people selling themselves, or injuring their children, to make them more appealing beggars. Africa gradually seeped into every pore of my soft, pampered, European skin and it will never leave me.

The Paris-Dakar was the most sweaty, hardcore, funny, pants-wetting dangerous job I have ever done - and I didn't spend a minute actually riding a motorbike. Not bad for a motorcycle journalist. I am forever grateful to BMW GB and Carole Nash Insurance, for letting me experience it just the once.

This book is intended to be much more than a race report, a chronicle of who fell off, or which team had the essential spare wheel bearings. It's the story of how a single trip changed my view of what motorcycling really means in the general scheme of things, and how fragile are the threads that bind us to any time or place.

Most people in the UK live in a sea of comfortable nothingness. Meanwhile a very different world without pensions, benefits, ready meals, iPads and every other modern convenience is just seven hours flying time away. In that cruel, bright sunshine world all you have are your family, and your tribe. Beyond that, you're on your own.

Some may get annoyed reading my story, some may smile. It is, in the end, just my version of events. My tiny grain of truth, scribbled in the dirt.

I hope that reading this inspires a handful of others to follow a less travelled road, to ride their motorbike over the next hill, just to see what's there. Life is a grey, repetitive desert when distilled into a mere workaday routine. We all need moments of joy, fear, wonder and the danger of navigating a strange, unearthly world.

Alastair Walker

CHAPTER ONE

PARIS, HOME OF THE RUDEST MOTHERS ON THE PLANET

It started with a chance remark at a Motor Cycle News (MCN) awards bash in exotic Birmingham. BMW GB motorcycles boss David Taylor casually asked me if I fancied doing the Dakar, as their regular guy, Mac MacDiarmid, had cried enough after doing three trips in succession.

As I was already necking the free house wine with a vengeance, naturally I said yes straight away, without even thinking about what the trip might actually entail. David laughed jovially at my instant enthusiasm - or gullibility, as it's known in bike journalism - then assured me he'd be in touch to `sort out the paperwork.'

That was pretty much the last I heard from old Dave, until we met up again at BMW's Bracknell office a few weeks later, to discuss the project in more detail. BMW were keen to get value from my trip, as it was costing them a cool £4500 to send me there. Carole Nash were also paying a month's wages, hotel bills, air fares, buying camping equipment, film, batteries blah-blah - about another £4000 worth of support.

For Carole Nash, this was a big deal, as the company had just launched insidebikes.com, one of the early online motorcycle magazines and they had earmarked a cool £100,000 for the first year's marketing budget.

BMW could see the chance to get a conventional feature out of my trip, plus some video footage, which they could use on their show stands. We'd already done a Cadwell track day launch with a tank-mounted camera on an R1100S and BMW liked the idea of making their bike brand look even more adventure-orientated with some authentic Dakar film of John Deacon in action.

Simon Pavey was also competing in the 2001 Dakar, aboard an F650 BMW and joined us at the meeting. Simon had done this event a few times before and had some excellent advice about surviving the whole Dakar experience. Things like, 'Don't trust the French,' 'hide your food and water whenever possible,' 'never be embarrassed about bribing people, it's how things get done on the rally.'

Aussie Si Pavey was a first class off-road racer, and a genuine no-bullshit bloke to boot, which is always a rarity in the UK bike industry. BMW also suggested I talk to Kevin Ash and Mac MacDiarmid, who had both covered the rally as BMW GB sponsored reporters. Mac MacDiarmid couldn't be arsed replying to my emails and phone calls, but the late Kevin Ash was more forthcoming.

In fact, Kevin was even more brutally honest than Simon and began to really scare me, as he described hair-raising landings at desert airstrips, gun-toting local gangsters circling the camps by night, the brain-sapping heat and the piss-poor facilities available in the press tent.

"Try and get fit, or at least lose some lard." advised Kevin, who had an accurate idea of my usual lifestyle from our occasional meetings on new motorcycle press launches. "Also, don't take the anti-malaria drugs, they'll probably just send you off your head...unless you like that sort of thing of course."

In addition, I asked some advice from my son-in-law - another Kevin - a Sergeant in the British Army, who had fought in the Gulf War some ten years previously.

"Try and stay hydrated especially in the middle of the day. I mean just drink f***ing gallons of water. It's so easy to get a bit crazy, saying and doing stupid things, because of the heat. Nobody from this country is used to it, but everyone thinks they can handle it. Three days without proper sleep soon sorts that shit out."

Somehow his advice carried more weight due to his hard-as-nails Scottish accent and the fact that he had most likely killed people.

I sipped a pre-rally training lager in the pub and asked Kevin what I should take in the tent, as I hadn't camped out for about 25 years.

"Big torch and a spare, in case the sand wrecks it, plus batteries, in fact take loads of `em. Batteries are good to trade with stupid people who only bring two. Get a small torch that straps on your head - good for packing, or setting up the tent in the dark. An air mattress is good if you've got space. Otherwise, try and sleep face down on your guts, as it's better than pressing your spine onto gravel each night. You need some shit roll and baby wipes - keep the sand out of yourself, it irritates your skin pretty quick. Thermals for night time, it can get un-fuckin-believably cold at night..."

I bought Kevin another beer. This was a job for mad people and I'd signed up for it - volunteered even.

****

Meeting John Deacon – BMW Rally Racer

Before the trip, BMW arranged a place for me at John Deacon's off-road school down in Cornwall, riding their F650 Enduro bikes, just so I could meet John before the rally.

JD, as he was known to most people in the strange sub-culture of enduro racing, was a giant, larger-than-life character and he was BMW GB's star rider in the Dakar that year. He was also one of the few Brit riders of his generation who were judged capable of a top three finish in the Dakar.

Of course, it's all the more poignant now because it turned out to be John's last Paris-Dakar, as he died competing in Syria, but had JD lived, I would still say he was one of the strongest, toughest, most naturally talented and resourceful, off-road riders I have ever seen. With a helping of luck, he could have won the event.

A small gaggle of journalists, some experienced, others muddy novices like me, had a tour of some lanes and tracks with JD, who was riding a stock, from the showroom, road going BMW R1150GS, with a 14 stone photographer riding pillion.

For those who don't know how big a Beemer R1150GS is, try to picture a motorbike made for giants, from huge metal girders, by the Tonka Toy company, then you'll get the general idea. It's frigging huge and it weighs about 600lbs with a full tank of gas. Yet John Deacon rode the thing through slime, across slippery grassy banks, popped the odd wheelie on it, like it was a Honda 125 Motocrosser - all whilst carrying a pillion passenger, who was busy snapping photos and changing lenses. Skill beyond words.

Deacon had competed in the Dakar a few times before of course, but this was his first year on the big 900cc factory BMW desert racing bike, which BMW Germany had built especially to try and trounce the effortlessly durable KTM 640 singles. The BMW twins had sheer, balls-out speed - but would they be as reliable as the orange KTMs?

Joan Roma, known as 'Nani' in off-road circles, was the star rider in the 2001 BMW squad, with John Deacon, American Jimmy Lewis and Frenchman Cyril Despres backing him up. In addition, a German lady rider, Andrea Mayer, was riding a factory BMW F650 single, hoping she had a shot at taking the women's title, within the motorbike class.

The whole thing was a very big deal for BMW that year, because they sold a large number of off-road GS motorbikes in their home country, and sales were rocketing in the USA, UK, Italy, France and elsewhere as the 1150GS impressed older riders with its brutally ugly, but gutsy charm.

BMW's big rivals in the Dakar were KTM, a small Austrian company, who were then probably about 20% the size of BMW in terms of financial strength in the world motorcycle market. But KTM held all the kudos with `true' off-road riders. In fact John Deacon was a KTM dealer, but he kept that very quiet whilst racing for BMW of course.

But you couldn't tell there was all this big money politics and factory team pressure, this Teutonic honour, weighing on John Deacon as we larked about down in Cornwall.

On the night before we rode the back lanes, he easily drank me under the pool table at the pub, constantly cracked jokes in his laidback Cornish burr and would occasionally refer to his BMW as `the old tractor.'

Yet there was an unmistakable, typically British quiet strength, a steely fire inside him, a real hunger to become the first ever Brit to win the Dakar. His eyes would focus somewhere outside the window when you asked him to recall dramatic incidents from Dakars gone by and he had a shrewd measure of how good, or how average, some of his rivals were.

"No names of course," he said over the journalist piss-up – sorry, I meant corporate evening meal, "but there's a load of convoy riding, a lot of follow-my-leader goes on. There's probably only five or six of us, when it comes to a sandstorm, who can genuinely read the GPS road book and have a crack at making a break from the rest."

Just to give us an idea of what a competition bike sounded like, John later started up the BMW F650 Dakar racer, which was parked in the hotel bar, and switched on the GPS satellite navigation, mounted above the handlebars.

"You're bombing along - on this baby Beemer that's about a ton flat out - and as you're dodging rocks and washes, you suddenly ride into this brown fog that starts sandpapering your face. Then, you have to see where the waypoints are on the GPS, aim for the right dune - all that shit - whilst keeping up some decent speed. I remember once seeing a rider about 10 feet in front of me just disappear, straight down a bloody big hole in the road, whilst I somehow just missed it. It's a right laugh."

Next day, I found out JD was right - following simple navigation, whilst on the move, was way, way harder than it looked.

Just trundling along after each other was fine, especially as we were all pootling through slushy English lanes at 30mph. But as soon as I was instructed to get to the front of the group and scroll our old fashioned, paper road books forward, whilst still trying to ride the bike, it all went tits up in about two junctions. I was utterly lost in a country with road signs, houses, trees etc. I had a million landmarks and reference points yet was lost within two junctions. Idiot.

It was so hard to simply concentrate on the F650 slewing about beneath me, watch out for tree branches about to decapitate me, or large rocks ready to pitch me over the handlebars, that I couldn't make sense of a single squiggle on the road book. My brain simply failed to process the extra information, even at such a slow speed.

For a brief moment, I tried to imagine what it would be like to ride 400 miles, in one day, across endless, identikit sand dunes, trying to keep the bike from ploughing itself into the rippling earth, whilst absorbing the fine detail on a GPS screen 18 inches from my nose.

That is one of those moments in life when you face up to your own distinct lack of true ability, for even after 25 years motorcycle riding experience you are hopelessly out of your depth. A tourist, not a competitor.

So now I began to understand what it took to simply enter this race, never mind finish 10,000 kilometres in three weeks.

****

The next few weeks flew by in a flurry of half-arsed preparations. I needed a full medical to get insured for the trip. Doctors and nurses smiled wryly as I told them what I was planning to do. A succession of some eight or nine tiny needles pumped vaccines into my arms, my diet improved and I started running three or four miles every other day, attempting to get semi-fit.

About 18 different forms, most of them written in badly translated French, were passed between myself, BMW and TSO (Thierry Sabine Organisation), who were the official organisers of the Dakar. Large sums of cash were spent by Carole Nash Insurance equipping me with 28 kilos (the maximum weight allowed per person) of gear to carry on my back for three weeks.

Obviously, I took a tent, sleeping bag, basic medical kit, clothing etc. but I also had a brand new Apple laptop, plus assorted cables, SLR camera, two lenses, batteries, flash unit, 30 odd rolls of slide film, (yes, this was pre-digital) Sony camcorder, more batteries, mini DV tapes, plus charge-up units, cables and continental electrical adapters. A notebook and pen was squeezed in too. The kit to do the journo thing weighed about 12Kgs - as much as all my personal belongings.

Finally, as part of my rigorous preparations, I had a very quiet time at the office Christmas party at work, drunkenly said goodbye to my family on Boxing Day, and emailed a fond farewell to anyone else I thought might care, if I died in a ball of flame somewhere near Bamako.

Army Sgt Major Kevin had recommended as short a haircut as possible to minimise the odds of various creepy-crawlies getting in my hair, so I also had my head shaved. A cold, nervous, middle-aged skinhead, headed for the airport just after Boxing Day 2000.

The adventure was beginning.

****

The flight to Paris was packed with regular people going for a New Year holiday in the French capital, so it felt great to intimidate them by taking off my bobble hat and peruse my SAS style survival book in the departure lounge. I was also dressed in one of those fisherman's gilet things, pockets packed with camera films (avoids repeated airport X-rays of your luggage) and a cheap, nasty pair of combat trousers from the local Army & Navy stores.

Oddly enough, very few people struck up any conversation with this would-be Big Issue vendor, although all the security staff seemed keen to invade my personal space, except for my butt-crack, thankfully.

After the usual dull flight, train ride and then a stupidly angry, Algerian road rage taxi ride to the centre of Paris, I arrived at £75 per night Hotel Renoir, which - as you might have guessed - was a kind of French impression of a decent hotel. Still, the lobby was nice.

Once checked in, I managed to squeeze myself and my luggage inside the tiny hotel lift, which was approximately the size of an old British red telephone box, but featured three mirrors to make you think it was Dr. Who's Tardis. I lurched to a sweaty halt on the third floor and tried to get into my room, but the key wouldn't turn properly. I jiggled it some more, swore a bit and the door opened – it shouldn't have done so, because my room was actually the room across the way.

A stunningly beautiful North African woman greeted me, wearing a very tight combo of jeans and T-shirt.

"Oui?" she said, giving me a suspicious look.

Then as I tried to reply in mangled Franglais, an angry North African man appeared from behind me, carting a suitcase.

"Er, sorry, there seems to be a mix up with the rooms." I said, standing there with the key to their room in my hand.

"What's this - f***ing some other guy already then?" said the geezer to the woman, who began waving her arms and talking at 90mph in French. Or possibly Angry Algerian. It was hard to tell.

After a few seconds of frenzied negotiations, the couple seemed to settle things, and then the angry fella shoved me backwards against the wall, kicked my bag at me, and then offered me some polite, yet accurate instructions;

'Listen M'sieur, f*** off back to where you came.'

Yep, I was in Paris alright. City of lights, city of lovers and the world centre for the rudest, most unpleasant, arrogant and unhelpful mother****ers I have ever known.

And that's just the taxi drivers.

****

CHAPTER TWO

THE SHOWBOAT STAGES

Next day was spent chasing about trying to find the Dakar Parc Ferme check-in area, getting lost on the Metro, filling in more bits of paper, being insulted in French and eating agreeable baguettes. I also received the official press kit from TSO, which was 98 pages long and weighed about 2 kilos. Cheers. You could have put it all on a CD maybe?

I then got changed into my lightweight desert combat pants, which made me look like some gay Backstreet Boys fan, donned my woolly hat and went to the official Dakar press call at a fancy hotel.

This turned out to be all pretty dull, with the entire proceedings conducted exclusively in French, a baffled assembly of mechanics, riders and support staff standing about trying to translate bits and pieces, and the final insult; the wine was piss poor.

However, I met up again with John Deacon and some of the BMW GB team, so it was nice to have a conversation in English. John was his usual cheery self and after a chat, I went back to the hotel, wrote up a report for the Carole Nash web magazine, *insidebikes.com* and then painfully uploaded it into the news section. It took hours to accomplish. Back in those days French internet connection speeds were similar to a rural 2CV overloaded with contraband meat products, and driven by a blind drunk farmer.

Because uploading one photo took about 20 minutes on a copper wire, when I went to check out of the salubrious Hotel Renoir early on New Year's Day, there was a problem; the massive phone bill.

The night porter/pimp/receptionist stared in disbelief at the bill for `Le informatique service,' and we agreed a price of about £120 for about six hours web time.

Having packed and paid the bill, I waited in the lobby for the taxi, which would take me to Le Bourget airport, and the start of my Paris-Dakar adventure. Naturally, it was late, being New Year's Eve. My pimp friend on reception, now happy that lots of cash had been paid for internet usage, phoned the taxi company again and shouted at them. For those who have never visited Paris, I can say that this is the ONLY way to get things done urgently.

Finally, a surly cab driver arrived in the usual Merc 190 diesel, complete with more dents than an iron bedstead in a bondage dungeon. I started to panic that I'd miss the Dakar before making the start. There was a hair-raising drive across Paris, dodging drunks waving fireworks, happy Parisians celebrating 2001 by hurling bottles of piss at each other, or attempting to make love to random strangers in the streets. I made Le Bourget at 4.55am. Exactly five minutes before the deadline.

But guess what? The deadline for the press plane was all bullshit by TSO anyway, because the press flight did not take off at 5.45 as the TSO instructions stated. Nope, it was a full hour later when we actually got on board the four engine, propeller-driven, Fokker aircraft.

In fact, I was the first journalist at Le Bourget and sat on my own like a dipstick, whilst more experienced people left it until the last minute to arrive. In any case, the plane wasn't going anywhere until the French TSO staff and `star' sports journos from L'Equipe and other French magazines arrived. Of course, they were all hammered from all night parties, so all us mugs from Japan, UK, Poland, Italy and everywhere had to wait. And wait. In the end, we took off about 7 a.m.

The 28 kilo personal luggage limit was another crock of shit too. You could actually take as much stuff as you liked, so long as you were French of course. The amount of kit that French radio people had with them was ridiculous - you could have filled eight seats with it and started broadcasting Radio Luxembourg again.

The Danish pilots of the Fokker were furious about this flagrant overloading of the aircraft. They insisted the baggage hold was repacked to balance the aircraft because of the French radio teams' three metric tonnes of kit.

Also, all the French journalists were given official Dakar jackets, T-shirts, combat trousers, caps etc. whilst foreign scum like myself received diddly squat. Naturally, nobody spoke to me, they just grunted, or sniggered, at my lame attempts to converse in GCSE grade D French.

But then, we boarded, fell over each other's equipment, met the agreeable Danish female air crew, and set off in the freezing Paris rain down the runway, wings vibrating as the turbo prop motors groaned at max thrust. This was it, I was on the Dakar and with a single step into the night air, and I was on a wild adventure to the Sahara.

Bon chance and au revoir, you Parisian mothers.

****

European Vacation

Stages 1-3 on the Dakar that year were `showcase' mini features, whereby all the vehicles would race around some little sections of dirt road, just to keep the sponsors happy and show the event off to keen spectators, mainly in France.

It was only when we had landed near Le Chatre in the middle of France and the coach was ferrying us towards the little motocross circuit where the special, timed stage would take place that morning, that I realised how much of a stupendously big deal the Dakar was – and still is - for the French nation.

Hundreds of people, no, make that thousands of `em, lined the roads. This was at eight-thirty in the morning, on January 1st don't forget, all there to cheer on anyone who looked like they were in the rally, or part of the support circus.

Placards with `Bon Chance,' or `Courage Mon Amis' had been made, people from aged eight to eighty were standing in the rain smiling. It really got to me, because in 25 years of following motorcycle sport in the UK I have never seen anything like it and I don't believe I ever will. That's because the British non-biking public regard bike racers as speed-crazed fools, not heroes.

****

The small 2km track at La Chatre had a few jumps on it, some tight turns and one decent straight, so I pitched myself near a jump and grabbed a few pics, plus some video clips, as the bikes went smoothly by. Nobody was trying too hard obviously, except for Richard Sainct (KTM) and Joan Roma (BMW), who both had their bikes sideways on each turn, showboating to the crowd.

The 2001 Dakar rally was shaping up to be a real clash between the Spaniard Roma, and last year's winner, Frenchman Richard Sainct, who had the look of a school Head Prefect about him and spoke very rarely and very concisely. Sainct was introverted and intense, Roma more passionate. Like all sporting rivalries it was very much a battle of personalities, as much as machinery.

The bikes went past, then the cars, and finally the trucks, or 'camions,' which I wasn't really bothered about. So I went into the press/crew marquee, where a bit of lunch was on offer - very welcome, as the outside temperature was about 4 degrees and windy. Local chefs and farmers had prepped the food, which was excellent and there was free red wine - ces't bon baby!

All very agreeable, but later on I had to use what was laughingly called the toilet facilities, which consisted of about 10 plastic portaloos near the track. Now bear in mind, there had been a couple of thousand spectators visiting the special stage that day already, including one young French couple I observed visiting 'trap four' simultaneously. Classy.

It goes without saying that apart from the foul stench and general New Year's Day bad aiming going on, there was no paper...so I improvised with the French language press releases. You see, a press kit can be useful!

So, late in the afternoon, we lined up in the dark, trooped back on the coach, and chugged slowly to the airport, which looked like some kind of abandoned chemical weapons plant by the way. The Fokker crew then carefully loaded the luggage, then took some off again, argued with the noisy French journos, and then finally balanced it again.

I should explain here why the crew did this.

For those who haven't travelled on small propeller aircraft, rather than commercial jets. The Fokker 27 needed the huge amount of heavy camera, radio equipment, plus all personal belongings stashed in a precise, balanced way, or there was serious risk of us running out of runway on take-off, or crash landing, nose first. It was really all about the handling of the aircraft, our safety basically, but there was much grumbling and snorting from the French journos who couldn't grasp what the problem was exactly.

All this pissing about delayed us but there was a good reason for that - the atrocious weather conditions near Perpignan - our next destination. The Danish crew asked Marie-Christine-Lamy, the Dakar Press Co-ordinator, to ask all French journalists to assist with re-packing the hold. Most of them refused. A handful, to their credit helped the rest of us redistribute the equipment safely.

This selfish behaviour continued at each stopover on the rally. There's a guy from a leading French newspaper who will get beaten - I mean really, savagely beaten to a bloody pulp - if I ever see his arrogant, bone idle face again in this lifetime.

Otherwise, we were all happy campers and getting along really well.

We were scheduled to stay that night in Narbonne, an historic French town near the border with Spain, with a landing at Perpignan.

As we got down to about 2,000 feet, the winds became stronger, plus we made a wide turn against the mountains to line our plane up for the landing approach. The Fokker was creaking, things kept ominously thudding about in the luggage bays, and I was out of my seat a few times, as we dropped into air pockets.

Luckily, I love flying, so none of this drama bothered me. But Brit photographer Neil, who was covering the rally for the Mitsubishi car team, was getting visibly agitated as the engines coughed and the French journos made `Whoa' noises near the front of the plane.

It was whilst the plane bucked and bounced, that I negotiated a deal with Neil, to use some of his rally pics in Carole Nash publications, in return for some beer money, plus shared accommodation in Narbonne and Castellon (Mitsubishi hadn't provided him with anywhere to stay at those stages, nice of them eh?). Top man that he is, he agreed instantly.

By the time we arrived by coach in Narbonne, it was eleven at night and all of us were utterly shattered. The bus dropped a small group of us near a hotel which was described as `student type chambres' by one of the TSO people. I would describe it as a category B prison.

Neil, myself, a French photographer and a couple of journos from elsewhere all wandered into the lobby of what appeared to be a 1950s French Foreign Legion outpost, run by squint-eyed Algerians. Paint hung off the walls, in layers of peeling history. The owner's wife - OK, possible female companion - cackled and muttered in French as we negotiated room rates. Let's face it, it was this, or pitch our tents in the street outside.

"Cent-onze francs M'sieur, une personne, une nuit." said the hotel guy, at least I think he said 110 Francs for a night, which is what I paid for me, and another 110 for Neil's room. It was only after cash had been paid that the owner's laughing receptionist informed me that we were sharing a room, at that rate. As that was about eleven pounds each, I wasn't expecting much. We didn't get it.

In the room there was a blinding 60 watt bare bulb hanging from the ceiling, which had several polystyrene tiles missing, exposing various pipes and electrical cables. The toilet, which was located in the middle of the room, had no seat, no lid and there was brown liquid already in there.

No paper, naturally - this was France after all, certain traditions remain sacred.

A rank, damp bed, with a pillow the thickness of a kebab pitta bread, awaited my weary head. Ciggy burns in the solitary, wafer thin blanket. No carpet, just stained linoleum on the floor. A sink lurked in the corner, but the hot tap wouldn't budge. The cold one trickled all night however.

Although I was knackered, I immediately agreed with Neil's suggestion that we go to the town centre, find a bar and get a bite to eat, plus a drink. This turned out to be a good move, as Narbonne is a quiet, slightly run-down place, but friendly enough and the beer was good. Those five bottles or so took the edge off the horror of our surroundings and we slept for a few hours.

A mere four hours sleep later, on a bed which contravened the Geneva Convention, we were up, and off on the coach to Chateau Lastours, for special stage two.

****

Ah Yes, The Mysterious Time Penalty Ploy M'sieur

The showcase Lastours stage was high in the hills and reached via a three hour coach journey from Narbonne. I was starving when we arrived for the `very good breakfast' we were promised, which was a croissant and coffee each. Wow. TSO you are spoiling us with this lean cuisine.

Lastours was a bad stage for John Deacon on the BMW 900, as its electrics died about ten feet from the start line, and he received a 30 minute time penalty for riding backwards on the course. In fact, he simply rolled downhill, then stood aside whilst others took their turn riding the route, but seeing as he was British, not French, the Dakar organisers stuck to the letter of the law on this `safety offence.'

So, John would start the race 30 minutes from the back when it reached Morocco. It's hard to imagine what that must feel like to a competitor who has spent most of their adult life working towards doing the Dakar, to be treated so childishly by the organisers, but all credit to John Deacon, he didn't hit anyone, or even raise his voice, when he must have been absolutely seething inside.

The stage ended for me with a bit of spectating, as the cars and trucks looped around the edge of the car park. Incredibly, a few nutters rolled their cars, one crashing out of the event because of heavy damage. They had just blown the thick end of £40,000 to enter the rally and were on their way home before getting a sniff of Africa. Depressing stuff.

But not as boring as the two hour coach ride back to Perpignan, the flight to Valencia, then another coach to Castellon. Again, it became a 19 hour day, as we finally checked into a hotel by midnight, after a big squabble in reception, caused by the French journos refusing to queue. I had a room booked over a month previously, so it was deeply satisfying to see much hand-waving and foot-stamping from the homeless French, and then calmly receive my reserved room key. Ah, luxury.

Also, we learn that we have a relaxing day ahead tomorrow, as the Spanish motorbike association has fallen out with TSO over cash, so the bike special stage, due to be run on the seafront, has been suddenly cancelled.

Excellent - a day on the piss then.

****

Next morning, I decide to wander down to the beach, just to take some pics anyway. I've missed the shuttle bus, but bump into Mitsubishi car racer Fontenay and his crew in the hotel lift, so I ask - in French - for a lift, jokingly of course. A look of pure contempt and stony silence is all I get in return. Talk about race face.

So I get a taxi instead and pay with a £20 sterling note, which the driver doesn't really want, but it's worth twice the actual fare. He shrugs and eventually accepts it.

After an hour watching the cars and trucks larking about in the man-made sand dunes on the beach, snapper Neil and myself head off for lunch in the town centre. It was hard to find anything open, being midday in winter and of course Spanish beach towns don't really open for business in January.

So we explore on foot, ending up in a backstreet bar, which is run by a kind of Catalan Bet Lynch character; all heaving bosom, purple eye-shadow and leopard skin pants.

She's cackling away with a bored sales rep, sitting at the end of the little bar, whilst we neck San Miguels and stare out of the window at passing traffic. Bizarre Latino disco/salsa music oozes from the radio as this odd couple flirt with each other in that base, really animalistic way, which middle-aged swingers are keen to do. Just as she drapes a leopardskin-clad leg across the bloke's toreador trousers, we decide it would be wise to move on.

The afternoon drifts pleasantly by and the beers increase.

We start saying stuff like `Scorchio' and `Excusez madam, vouz aimer ma chapeau?' at random women as they pass our cafe bar table. Thankfully, nobody takes serious offence at this typically British lager lout behaviour. The fact that both of us look like unshaven, garden shed tramps, recently thrown out of a bail hostel, also helps ward off any human contact.

Late to bed, a drunken phone call home, then sleep. Tomorrow, we have to be up at 5.30am, for we're on our way to Africa. I check the press kit schedule and read the brief notes on this first stage of the `proper' Dakar rally, as it enters Morocco.

I say the name, Er Rachida, slowly inside my head, trying to picture what the place will be like.

****

CHAPTER THREE

IRON COLD MOUNTAINS AND LE HERC

Touchdown at Er Rachida, a military airfield in the Atlas Mountains.

It's warm, like an English summer's day, with thin cloud just breaking up at 9 o'clock in the morning. Nobody says anything, so I watch what the French journos do, which is pitch their tents close to the aircraft, parked on a huge Tarmac apron, some 200 metres off the runway.

French TV uses a massive Hercules transporter plane, which acts as the main gathering point for the tented village which huddles beneath its awesome wingspan. The call it `Le Herc' and it makes a spectacular sight in the sunshine, its giant arm draped yards and yards over the edge of the runway, casting a welcome shadow.

If you are a bit of a plane spotter, there are all sorts of aircraft on this rally to delight your little red Silvine notebook.

Lumpy looking, droopy snouted Russian Antonovs ferry cargo, and there's a Short Brothers' `Bumble Bee' Skyvan, (which really is the Luton box van of the air), or how about a Twin Otter? There's a couple of Fokkers, plus a small fleet of Squirrel helicopters - in total, there are twenty-seven aircraft transporting bits of this off-road circus around North-West Africa.

Fascinated, I spend an hour or so just wandering around taking photos of the aircraft. Getting squinty-eyed and red-faced in the African sun, it feels like I'm on the ultimate school trip.

Then, after making a long, complicated job of pitching my
'one touch' tent for the first time, I grab my camera and go on
a trek to the bivouac, which is maybe a kilometre from the
main Parc Ferme area, along a gravel track. I am in need of
food, as it's been about six hours since breakfast.

Once I slowly trudge down the road in my new hiking
boots, getting well away from the rally, there is very little noise
and my eyes squint into the distance, trying to take in the
vastness of the landscape which envelops me. The mountains
rise three, maybe thirteen miles away. It's difficult to tell. The
peaks have an almost Martian aspect; sharp edged, and tawny-
beige in the sunlight. Stones poke through my boots, because
the ground is flint hard, unyielding.

Morocco isn't the sandy Sahara some people imagine
from movies or TV, or at least the bit near Er Rachida isn't. It
has a harsh, broken tooth edginess to it, a kind of lunar
coldness which I found odd, unsettling. It's as if people don't
really belong in this brutal, jaggedly empty topography, instead,
it was created for scorpions.

****

But the bivouac was worth the walk. It was more than the
wedding style marquee I'd been expecting. A loose, billowing
square of canvas awnings and Moroccan carpets surrounded
the French catering trucks, with cloth-covered serving tables
inside and a well-stocked bar. Yep, you can buy beer tokens on
the Dakar - boy, have they got journalists sussed at TSO…

Lunch was excellent, washed down with Kronenbourg 1664
and I began to feel optimistic, really excited, about the three
week trek around North West Africa which lay ahead. This
would be fun, inspiring and different from anything I'd ever
done. All of which was true. But after doing some interviews

late in the afternoon, and then having an agreeable evening meal, things began to unravel a tad.

Firstly, it proved impossible to hook up my Mac to the internet, which - according to the press info blurb from TSO - was perfectly possible, so long as you paid vast sums in phone time. I had already signed for an open ended account with TSO back in Paris to obtain the phone time, so in theory, it should have been no sweat.

But in reality, you had to write copy, save it to a PC format disk, not a Mac, and then ask the IT guys - in French - to kindly send it via satellite link, when they felt arsed. Oh yeah, and could they please simply guesstimate how long it took, then add on twenty francs, so that the maximum call charge could be levied to my foreign scum company/publisher? Merci Monsieur. That bullshit just took me about three hours, to send a short report which I typed up in 20 minutes. Jobsworth IT F**kers.

It was lucky that I'd bribed my photo buddy Neil with Dakar beer tokens, so that I could use his old skool PC laptop, plus floppy disks, instead. Basically I'd brought along a Mac laptop worth about £1000 which was now a handy sandstorm paperweight. Deep joy.

All this shilly-shallying meant it took until midnight for both of us to file a race report, which we had typed up by about 8pm that evening. But obviously, all French journos got first use of the limited plug sockets, internet connection time etc.

Now we had another problem; the temperature. After sunset, you could see your breath as you exhaled in the press tent. By midnight, you really needed fingerless gloves to type properly, or maybe do sit ups between paragraphs. One of the aircraft crew wandered past, wearing a coat that Chris

Bonnington might have chosen for an attempt on Everest, and cheerily told me it was now minus 4 degrees Celsius. I jogged across the Tarmac towards my tent.

Despite putting on virtually all the clothing I had with me, then wriggling inside my sleeping bag, donning my woolly hat and leaving just a two inch breathing hole in the zipped up sleeping bag, my feet were numb. Actually even my knees were numb. Only the four cans of beer, plus some red wine which I had necked in the press tent, helped sent me to sleep for a few hours. I awoke just after three a.m.

It was probably lucky that the booze caused me to stir, desperate for a piss, because otherwise hyperthermia could have set in.

Outside, it felt like one of those dark, winter, permafrost nights from my North of England paper round youth. The air tasted funny, thinner, sharp as lime as you took it down into your lungs. People were huddled near the planes, or yellowy generator-powered mechanics lights, trying to feed off any source of heat, no matter how slight.

I pulled my sleeves down over my frozen fingers and staggered sleepy-eyed to the embers of a fire about 150 metres away from the planes, stamping life back into my dead toes. Three or four blokes were near the flames, but nobody really spoke. We all grunted at each other and rubbed our own hands and faces, as if we could wash this invisible, chilblain pain away.

My whole body felt heavy with fatigue and cold, knees creaking as I fidgeted near the orange and black lumps of wood. I couldn't really think straight, I began to wonder if I was really awake, or having a dream of some sort.

The cold was surreal. It froze the sleepy glue at the corners of my eyes.

I hated the Dakar now; this airport, the thin Atlas altitude, this empty corner of jagged dry land, peppered with icy glinting stars above me.

"Does anyone know when the sun rises?" I asked. No answer, nobody spoke English.

"La soleil, retournez; a qui heur?" I mumbled instead.
"Tres heures, possible." Came a muttered reply.

"Fuckin' hell."

The fire died down. I went back into my tent, sat scrunched up in the sleeping bag, ate some food, and talked to myself. Didn't sleep. Those were the longest, coldest, hardest three hours of my life. I found out later that the temperature dropped to minus 9 just before dawn.

Next time I saw a homeless person in winter, I knew why they drank. You'd drink anything, absolutely anything to dull that pain.

****

We had a fairly early flight slot to our next stop, so it was just after dawn as I burnt my tongue against a steaming hot chocolate drink in the bivouac, then wolfed down an assortment of snacky breakfast foods.

After building up some body heat by packing up the tent and all my gear, I was feeling human again, as we sat on the plane, ready to fly about 40 minutes to Ouarzazate, which sounded pretty exotic, romantic even.

"Ou-zaar-zatee." I said to myself as the Fokker leaned into a tight turn, while the pilot weighed up the airstrip below. There were more mountains nearby, but the runway was good, smooth Tarmac. It was a soft, almost package holiday type landing.

Once off the plane, I could see this was another Moroccan military base, like Er Rachida. The altitude was lower however, so it felt reasonably warm when we touched down. Hopefully it would be warmer at night.

The setting wasn't as Spartan as Rachida. Here, we had a mini street market laid on for us, a few more Moroccan military Police and armed guards mooching about, plus a toilet block. The toilets inside were a row of filthy holes in the ground, with those crazy French pedals for your boots naturally, but it was better than digging in the desert.

****

I caught up with John Deacon in the afternoon at BMW's pits and he wasn't in a good mood. The time penalty in France had put him out of contention - barring some freak accident befalling the top ten runners - and he knew it. Also, he had picked up a £750 speeding fine today, after being radar trapped going through a village too fast.

"Fair enough," grumbled John, " Nobody wants to see someone being run over whilst they're waving at us, but if I was speeding today, and still struggled to make up five minutes time on Richard (Sainct) and the leaders, then how fast were they going?"

Morale wasn't good in the BMW camp, even at this early stage. I could sense the frustration and the tension between all their riders. Jimmy Lewis, the US dirt bike specialist, arrived later in the Parc Ferme, after crashing heavily. His wrists were visibly swelling and that jabbing, broken bone pain, that motorcycle riders know too well, was written all over his face.

They helped him off the bike gingerly. Jimmy knew the race was over for him, it was an early exit, caught by the snaggly teeth of Moroccan trails.

Within minutes, Jimmy was slumped against the BMW truck, and just left alone by the crew. Nobody helped him to get medical attention, or offered all-important psychological comfort, social contact - the invisible glue of any competitive team. Deaks and Cyril Despres, barely said more than two sentences to Lewis, or to each other. Joan Roma was in his tent, seemingly exhausted.

By contrast, BMW Team Manager Bertie H is relatively jovial, but efficient, concentrating on barking orders, getting the bikes checked and fixed up for tomorrow's onslaught of sand, gravel and stones. Just a few days into the race and the blue BMWs already look scarred, beaten with sticks almost. This is a tough race, no question.

Despres doesn't speak to me, doesn't even look at me. Just stares into the distance, as if auditioning for some French noir thriller movie. I take a few photos and make my way elsewhere as the riders drink water and relive the race stages behind tired eyelids.

But later on, when I hang around the KTM pits, doing some more photos, I immediately notice an entirely different atmosphere. Every little thing is being done for Sainct, the French number one, to give him a shot at winning. Water, as soon as he arrives, is passed to his grateful hand, then a cold towel. After that, a crew member helps Richard get his boots off.

This is a total contrast the BMW team, where everyone seems to be doing their own thing. KTM have a proper rider debrief, people make notes as the riders talk. Even lesser, semi-factory KTM team riders are being quizzed on how they rode that day, what they saw, who can act as a pace-setter tomorrow etc. The general speed and work rate of the KTM crew is simply snappier, keener, than BMW.

Semi privateers like Per Lundmark, are being loaned KTM factory tools and allowed to camp near the KTM lorry, such is the Austrian factory's determination to dominate this rally, by sheer weight of numbers. This is a family atmosphere almost, and I feel certain that KTM will win this race. The Austrians also have another ace in the pack - Alfie Cox.

Cox is a jovial, South African enduro racer who lives and breathes this event - and lets it show all day long. His dry, sarcastic banter never stops, his wolfish smile flicks out from under his baseball cap all the time. Alfie knows almost everyone who counts on the rally and he has a kind of music hall spiv brand of moustachioed charm.

Whilst school prefect Sainct is hard work to talk to - very taciturn, insular, and unwilling to say anything unless he absolutely has to - Cox is the social lubricant in the KTM team engine. He entertains, he inspires, and makes this dangerous, crazy racing seem lighter, more fun than it has any right to be.

BMW haven't got anyone to match that driving personality, which is a real weakness on an event where mental attitude, psychological strength, is far more important than having an extra ten bhp from your engine.

****

At night, the locals put on a bit of a cabaret near the main bivouac fire, which is set in the middle of the tented square. Women dance and make that strange yodelling noise they use to summon the spirits of sundown. Musicians use an assortment of parping woodwind and jangling percussion to keep everyone's toes tapping. Like folk music everywhere in the world, it was mostly an appalling racket, performed by people who should never be allowed to give up their day job.

The heat of the fire was welcome though. The food was excellent too and after a few beers I borrowed Neil's phone to ring home. There were few stars visible that night, as thin cloud had drifted over, but the spin-off was a spectacular, hazy sunset, colouring the mountains burnt ochre and purple.

For a while, as the shadows wrapped us and the sparks swirled skywards, Ou-zaar-zatee looked beautiful to me.

****

Next day we pack up and move on to a place called Goulimine. Something very weird happens here; it rains. Yep, a few drops of drizzle fall from the flat, grey sky in the afternoon and it feels a little bit cold. It's an odd glimpse of winter that's followed us down here.

The racers enjoy the un-Sahara type conditions and set a fast pace, with Roma winning the 370 kilometre stage, followed by a posse of KTM riders, and BMW's Despres in 10th, who falls off just before the end of the stage, putting a huge dent in his front wheel rim. Jimmy Lewis finishes the stage in an incredible 13th place, with his hands and wrists visibly swollen from his injuries yesterday.

"The doctors say nothing's broken, just badly beat up, twisted 'em badly...but it hurts like hell to use the clutch, so mostly, I didn't bother." says Lewis, who almost runs over an official as he arrives at a checkpoint, completely unable to pull the clutch in. You'll probably get a time penalty for that Jimmy…

John Deacon is making up time now and has inched his way into 30th place on the leader board, but JD remains a couple of hours behind Sainct, who leads the bike rally. In truth big John is simply making up the numbers now, it would take a miracle for him to close up by 2 hours.

Yet at lunchtime (yep, the top riders all finished 370 kilometres of 90mph off-road racing by 12.30-ish) Deaks is exchanging crude banter and saucy remarks with Alfie Cox, who is celebrating his birthday today.

"F*** me Alfie, that was fast out there today - surprised you didn't use your bus pass mate, take it easy."

"Still finished 5th John and that's about 20 places ahead of you. All those pies slowing you down mate, or did you stop for a quick leg over on the way this morning?"

"Hey, what goes on the tour, stays on the tour..." says Deaks, as the KTM and BMW pit crews smile at the two friends winding each other up. It's good to see everyone relaxing a little bit in the bivouac tent - not something you would ever see Honda or Yamaha racers doing at a motorcycle GP, or Superbike event, that's for sure.

The Dakar is a serious business. People can, and still do, get hurt, or killed out here. To emphasise the potential danger, race director Hubert Auriol holds a press call in the afternoon and informs us that the Polisari - a local faction keen on having their own slice of Morocco - have issued a formal warning that the rally has `no authorisation' to pass through their controlled area.

"This means we have to be careful, as they may attack, or more likely have laid mines for us." says Auriol calmly. I remain calm too.

Because I'm travelling by plane, not on four or two wheel. Just like Msr Auriol

The bizarre thing about the Dakar is that few people take much notice of such warnings. Africa is a dangerous continent, yet the spirit of adventure, the adrenaline rush of waking up and seeing a cinemascope landscape before you, pushes the fear into a tiny corner of your mind.

On the road to the bivouac that evening, I meet a married couple, tourists, who have followed the rally down from England, through France and Spain, then into Morocco in their VW camper van. They've brought along their new born baby too, just a few months old. They are having a great time, escaping the damp, dreary misery of Britain in January, seeing something epic in motorsport and loving every moment of their adventure.

I wish them luck and join the queue for food. Africa teaches you one thing; risks are everywhere, and life is fragile thing which sometimes exists by the grace of others, or sheer luck. So go with your instincts, enjoy. You never know what lies around the corner.

Wrapped up in dirty clothing, sipping beer and swapping unlikely stories around the spitting firelight, I never felt so alive, so aware that we're all on an unknowing journey - every spark and atom of us - from here to somewhere else.

****

Onwards we go then, to a small town called Smara.

This place is a small garrison town, an old Foreign Legion outpost, with the rally safely corralled onto the fringes of the military airport and the town itself, just half a mile or so away past the end of the runway. This is a disputed part of Morocco as it was once a Spanish territory and there is a different feeling here from Ouarzazate – no dancers, no drums. Just locals staring at us with hard eyes from beneath their desert headgear.

Ours is one of the first aircraft to touch down that morning and I join the French TV crew in pitching our tents near the massive Hercules. This will prove to be a mistake in just under 24 hours.

After dozing for a while in the tent, before the heat of the day becomes too much, I ask around and discover that the bivouac is set up inside what looks like some old barracks, which are complete with a shower block. The cost of a cold shower is just ten francs, or about a pound in UK cash, which is irresistible to me. I grab my minimalist shower/washing kit, some clean underwear and trek over, along with Neil. Neither of us have had a shower since Spain.

Once at the block, I'm nice and sweaty after walking across a hot, windswept airstrip, but instead of a Butlins type shower hut, all I can see are piles of rubble, vaguely fashioned into what looks like a row of open plan, Burtons changing rooms.

The whitewashed walls are wide open, offering a full view of all the naked Europeans as they shower. There's much amusement from the snaggle-toothed, 70 year old, all-male shower operators, as they check out our lily-white buttocks and lobster pink, sunburnt arms and noses. The showers themselves are simply rubberised bags of water, dangling from a pole, with a sprinkler valve attached.

You pay the strangely over-friendly, and constantly laughing cash man a few Cfa (a local franc related Moroccan currency) at each cubicle, turn the tap on – and bingo. Total refreshment and German style naturism to boot.

My operative spoke French and after trying to rip me off for double the going rate, we agreed a pound for `la mini douche' and he promised to watch my stuff whilst I got soapy for the Moroccan massive. I would say that about 30 percent of the townsfolk had lined up to spectate and/or pinch anything of value left lying around by the white-assed bathers.

I have to admit to feeling like I was in some gay porno prison movie, as a leather-faced bloke grinned at my white ass and made small talk in his local dialect. Could have been death threats, I really had no idea. However, despite dropping the soap a few times - not deliberately I have to say, it was a very small bar for economy reasons - nobody made any sort of move on me, or ran off with my finest Millets outdoor clothing. The clothes did contain all my money and passport, so that was good.

Feeling loads better about life in general after the first shower in three days, Neil and I then headed to the food queue, grabbed some excellent lunch, plus beers, and found a spot of shade to waste time in, until the bike racers were due to arrive.

We got talking to an unfeasibly tall British guy called David Singer, who seemed to have something to do with the chartering of various jets on the rally, mainly Russian Antonovs. David had been on a few Dakars and told us some funny, and scary tales from years gone by.

"It's a safer trip nowadays for sure." explained David, "Once it was common for at least a dozen people to lose all their kit, money, passports - the lot. The thieving was well organised, but it's not so bad now. I seem to recall a car load of journalists getting killed for their cameras one year...mind you, that could happen in Cape Town, Bosnia...lots of places. The world is a dangerous place now."

"Why do they use those Antonov jets so much - just cheap to hire?" I asked.

"Well there is that of course, but the Antonovs are short runway planes, perfect for odd little landing strips. Good to fly too, tight turns are OK for them, crosswinds on the strip - all that stuff. Most of the crew are ex-Russian air force, mad as fish. Drink like `em too - they'll drink the bloody anti-freeze from the `planes."

"What?" I asked in disbelief.

"Well most of the anti-freeze is alcohol anyway…nah, I'm joking you. They wouldn't make booze from anti-freeze, just bring their own vodka. All great fliers anyway, top pilots - never make a second pass at landing, even in sandstorms."

"Hmmm, right."

I wasn't entirely sure whether David was just pulling our legs, because we were Dakar `virgins,' or if the screen wash drinking pilot stories were true. But our aircrew were Danish and looked very sensible, so that was OK with me.

****

The motorcycle racers arrive late in the day. Today was one of the longer stages on the rally and packed with rocky trails too. There have been breakdowns and small accidents, even Sainct and Roma got lost whilst battling for the lead.

Spaniard Esteve Pujol slipped through and took the stage win, with Italian rider Fabrizio Meoni in second spot. Sainct still leads the event overall however. I catch up with John Deacon in the BMW pits later.

"Tough day, took it easy really as I didn't want to crash on the rocks and lose more time. It will be easier for me to try and make some time back on the sandy stages later on, plus navigation counts for more out in the *real* desert too. The sandy stuff is different from these moon rocks. I kept passing people broken down, hoping they might be the leaders, but no luck...still a long way to go for all of us though."

The BMW camp looked fed up. Roma was pissed off at getting lost. Meanwhile Cyril Despres had shredded his rear tyre on the sharp rocks and finished 69th out of 90-odd riders. Not good and Despres had the grim-faced look of a man who had battled to keep his bike upright for about 100 miles, as it tried to spit him off.

German female BMW racer, Andrea Mayer, was currently lying in 94th place but seemed content with that. She really wanted to win the ladies class, but there was still plenty of mileage left for her to catch the few female rivals she had in the two wheeled class.

Good ol' Jimmy Lewis once again sat grimacing in pain, as his wrists throbbed, sweat pouring from him after the stage. I felt sorry for Jimmy, John, Cyril Despres and even Mayer, but as nobody really wanted to speak more than a few words, I buggered off to get a couple of beers whilst I filed a report. You can't interview demoralised people, they just want the misery to end.

Later on, I spoke with Brit privateer Mike Hughes, riding a Honda 400, and saw his hands, which were a Picasso-like montage of blisters. Typical Northern bloke Mike was in 89th place, but absolutely not bothered.

"All I want to do is survive. I once did a ride from Peking to London for Children In Need," said the Yorkshireman, "and the hardest part was nearly 3,000 miles of forest trails across Russian republics. Endless, fly infested, swamps...just miles of empty plains. That was hard but I made it. I'm just trying to make it to Dakar, that's all. The place I finish in doesn't matter a bit."

Mike had crashed 'loads' today, hitting big rocks, one of which had wrecked his front wheel, but he was fixing his XR400 up before getting ready for food and sleep. There was another big day for him tomorrow. His morale, even though he had no team members to support him whatsoever, seemed impossibly high. His hands seeped blood as he turned spanners, but he really didn't give a monkeys – he was on his own personal Everest. End of.

****

The next stage was one of those where TSO wanted riders and drivers to fail, so that there were fewer vehicles to ship back from Dakar. You see the TSO organisers had already booked far fewer container spaces for the return trip home – some vehicles were staying in Africa, by fair means or foul.

Today, the riders faced 628 kilometres of gruelling travel, taking the race to a place called El Ghallaouiya, which the French rally crew called `Alleluya,' which was basically a village tucked away in a horseshoe shaped, furnace of rocks, just across the border into Mauritania.

It was going to be a very big day, a real test for all the drivers and riders. Most people who could, got an early night in. Others had broken motorcycles to fix up. If you failed to make the start time slot, then you were out of the event.

Next morning, I got a bright and early start, just before five am. It was still dark, but there was no question of sleeping in. At first I thought I was having a weird dream, and then the electrical whirring turned into a growling, sonorous whoosh. The Herc was firing up an engine, to power the tailgate hydraulics as French TV packed up their gear.

By the time I'd got out of my sleeping bag, the racket was deafening, and a gale of fuel-enriched air was powering through my tent like a Moto Guzzi wind tunnel. Things began to move and I rapidly made the decision to physically drag the tent, with all its contents out of the raucous downdraught.

I slowly shook out my boots, in case scorpions or spiders had made a bed for the night inside, and then began hurriedly packing my stuff by torchlight. This was lucky, because just as I had emerged from the tent, and almost finished stuffing my rucksack full of loose clothing, my documents, spare food and a water bottle, they fired up the other three engines on the Herc.

The din now sounded like an approaching avalanche, and the ground shook as the Herc flexed its massive muscles. A wall of noise hammered around the airstrip and everyone was awake for miles around. Even Odin was banging his shoe in Valhalla telling them to keep the racket down. The Herc was obviously first in the slot for this morning flights.

Suddenly I was aware of the wind changing direction and the engines revving. Shit, they were leaving right now. Along with 50 others, I suddenly realised that our tents were still too close to the aircraft and once they started to taxi, the rudder-directed mini hurricane from four immense engines would sweep everything that wasn't nailed down away in a 100-odd metre jet wash.

"They're moving the Herc Neil - get up mate!" I yelled at my photo buddy, who had poked his head out of his tent.

"Great. The bastards could have mentioned it when we pitched here."

I just managed to get the tent down, and lay on it, clenching a fist around my rucksack, as the Herc finally closed its massive doors and began its taxi movements. A huge cloud of dust and assorted debris engulfed the straggling remains of the tented village that had slept beside the airplane all night.

My Dutch journo buddy Jan lost his Moroccan slippers, which danced away across the runway in the pitch darkness. The Japanese journalists, shocked awake but enduring the ordeal stoically, stood rigid, braced against their tents, having dragged them fifty metres back when all the engines fired up. The older Japanese journo had his white gloves on - we never saw him remove these gloves, except to eat - during the entire rally. Touch of class there.

Thick-headed with sleep deprivation and the after effects of five or six cans the night before, I – and many others - cursed the Herc and all its crew. Words can't describe how much of a ball ache it is having one of the world's biggest military transport aircraft as your early morning alarm clock, every morning, for over two weeks. But the French have a word for it;

Merde.

****

CHAPTER FOUR

WEIRD SCENES INSIDE MAURITANIA

Whilst the race headed for the remote waypoint of El Ghallaouiya, we press hacks, plus many other rally logistics, catering, medical crew etc. were all dropped off for a four day stopover at an old French Foreign Legion town called Atar.

There were some hotels in Atar, which most of the French journos and race organisational staff had already booked into for the duration of our stay. No crapping next to a runway for them, no sirree, although I'm sure many of them maintained the proud French tradition of simply urinating in the street whenever the urge took them.

Instead, we foreign scumbag journalists and photographers pitched our tents near the main security blockhouse at Atar airport, right next to the official press tent, which seemed the safest and most sensible option. Our Fokker was one of the first planes there, so I watched as other aircraft arrived. The Antonovs almost dropped from the air at the last second, and then did a handbrake turn at the end of the runway. It was impressive. Atar is quite a big airport, with plenty of hard standing and several planes parked up well away from the main runway, as this was a four day stopover.

Then mid-morning, I was astonished to see a glamorous, sleek Lear jet land and park up. This was BMW's corporate plane and although I sneaked a little peek at it later on, their staff forbid anyone to take pictures, or broadcast images of it on TV, in case it somehow upset their shareholders, or co-sponsors.

Some people, including BMW customers, might have thought it looked like BMW's corporate VIP guests were on the Dakar simply have an 80s style disco, with a lavish buffet and lashings of champagne, right in the middle of abject poverty, squalor and merciless government corruption.

Which they did later that evening. In fact a handful of suits had the techno beat cranked up load and were dancing on the airport apron, once the Liebraumilch really kicked in.

I was naturally a bit miffed that I didn't even get an invite, as BMW GB had paid for the press place, but anyway, I'd left my gold disco shoes at home due to baggage restrictions.

The west side of the Dakar camp at Atar was surrounded by the impoverished Mauritanians, the `blue people,' as the French called them. They looked at us with a slave trader's disdain, laughing at our white legs poking out of shorts. We were like turtles out of our shells; we didn't belong in this bright, burning desert.

Some locals bribed the guards and were allowed in to try and sell us souvenirs, sweets, canned drinks etc. Armed guards stood close by, in case the hungry people gathered at the fence broke through and made a rush for us. At first it was scary, but then you got used to it.

Intrepid Jan from the Netherlands announced to myself and my new friend Alberto, who worked for an Italian motorcycle magazine, that he was going to stay in a local family's house, for the price of a few francs, as `it seems a good chance for some adventure.' We wished him good luck.

Later on, Jan told us what his stay in this `guest house' was like;

"They lived in four walls, kind of made from clay, bits of wood, anything that would stay upright. No roof, a fire in the middle, few pots and pans, beds - that was it. Like many people, they have a few goats, there's hardly any work here for anyone to do. The saddest day was the second day I stayed there, because they killed the family dog, to make a special stew for the honoured guest."

"Oh God, Jan - did you eat it?"

"It would have been very rude not to have some. It tasted OK actually. I felt sorry for them all, so I gave them more money than the price of the stay, plus my pair of Levis - I think they were more impressed with the Levis than the money. Brand names are for the super-rich out here."

This last observation was definitely true. In every stopover on the rally, there were kids sporting crude, knock-off copies of designer label T-shirts with `Nikke' or 'Addidaz' logo scripts ironed on them. The genuine brand label had more power in Mauritania than local currency, as I found out when I chucked away my Calvin Klein undies and a guard asked if it was OK if he had them. I said `sure' and he was delighted, despite the fact that I'd worn them for four days straight.

But cash also works in staving off the slow, half-starved misery of existence for the locals too. Despite your best intentions to ignore it, and not choose someone as a cause, you end up giving money away. The guilt just gets to you in Africa. Every step you take you hear `Cadeaux, M'sieur, cadeaux,' relentlessly, endlessly.

There is no job seekers allowance here, no housing benefit, and no welfare state that we would recognise. Just work, or nothing. If your family, or tribe, will not help you in hard times, then you die. It really is that brutally simple.

This desperation drives people beyond begging. Hunger concentrates the mind to make tough decisions.

Peter, the German journalist, takes up someone's offer of a shared taxi ride to see Atar's market and the surrounding town centre. Later, in the bivouac, he looks shaken as he describes how he wandered the market square, his little group besieged by begging children, then he foolishly bought a bag of boiled sweets from a trader and threw handfuls into the air.

"A child bit off part of another child's nose in the vicious fighting. I have never seen anything like it, they were like dogs. It was horrible."

"We might all fight that hard to survive, if we had to. We might do anything. Eat each other, like some of our ancestors in Europe did. We just have the luxury of welfare nowadays, that's all that keeps us civilised." I added. There was a thoughtful silence around the bivouac.

The rally stayed overnight in `Alleluya' so there's little for us to do today. No vehicles check-in, no riders to interview. After the evening meal, and just before it gets dark, I suggest to Alberto that we wander along the runway and check out the aircraft. We take a couple of beers and watch the sky painted orange and red. The breeze rustles our open shirts.

Suddenly I notice a small group of people approaching from the long grass near the end of the runway. There's a guard with his gun slung over his shoulder, walking in front of two girls, both wearing headscarves and long dresses.

"AJ, what do they want, what is this?" asks Alberto.

The guard asks me in French if I need ` a friend for the night.'

I answer 'Non, merci M'sieur' and we start to walk away, but they come closer to us and the guard starts harassing Alberto. Alberto doesn't speak more than four or five words of French and asks them in English what they want. The guard gestures to the girls, and giggling they reveal their faces. One could actually be a young boy. Hard to tell.

The guard asks 'L'homme, la jeune fille M'sieur, c'est bon eh? Vingt-Cinque Cfa…jiggy-jiggy oui?

Alberto gets that bit and quickens his pace.

"No, it cannot be…this is very bad AJ."

I do my best in French to explain we are married – to women – and not interested. But they are persistent and of course the price drops 5 Cfa. The guard is all smiles, his arms outstretched and pleading for some kind of cadeaux. A small boy, maybe seven, eight years old is flicking a stick at a goat near the back of this enterprising group.

"OK, le prix speciale, si vouz plait…Cinque Cfa pour le chevre…merci M'sieur, merci."

I stop and stand still for a second or two as it sinks in. Yes, he really is offering me a quick one with a goat for five local francs – or about 50p. The realisation then sunk into my beer-fuddled brain that someone must have already done that; otherwise there wouldn't be a going rate for goats. God in heaven. We made a swift exit. In fact we ran back to the planes once I gave the guard about 2.50p and the dregs of my beer.

That is what true poverty means. Everything and everyone, is for sale. That is slavery.

****

Back at the press tent, there's a special bulletin posted on the noticeboard, which acts as a stark reminder to everyone that we are doing something dangerous here.

In a few perfunctory words, the news update describes how the rally has suffered a casualty today. A crew member from a Brazilian car team has lost his lower leg, after driving over a landmine near the infamous `wall of sand' – known to the riders as the berm - which is a marker in the Polisari-Spanish Sahara dispute.

Apparently, the driver left the main track to move out of the way of other support vehicles. He then drove his 4X4 over a mine, which blew one front wheel, some bodywork, electrics plus his foot and ankle tissue clean off. The rally organisers are keen to express regret, but they also mention that everyone was told to stay 100 percent on the route – no deviations - on that particular stage.

As the rally only issues briefings and statements to competitors and crews in French and English, I wonder if the unlucky driver spoke fluent English, or some French. If not, then how would a Portuguese speaking Brazilian have been informed of the specific dangers on the route that day? Psychic powers perhaps…the gift of mime maybe? Or maybe a cardboard sign with `Achtung Minen' scrawled upon it would have been useful at 5.45 am today?

The incident highlighted the basic communication problems on an event which has some 1300 people, from over 60 different countries, taking part. It would be impossible to give briefings in all the languages required, but even so, two languages in a sandpit of Babel is hardly trying very hard is it?

****

The first night at Atar was a strange one. And not just because I was offered goat action on the cheap…

I had been allocated a space on a little Twin Otter, 12-seater aircraft, to visit El Ghallaouiya for the following day, to see the `yacht loop' stage, as it was nicknamed. The rally would do a simple 500 kilometre triangle in the desert, easy as that. We were due to fly at daybreak, so I went to bed early. If I was late, the plane wouldn't wait for me, so Marie-Christine informed me at the Press Office.

A generator powering the press tent rattled away some 20 feet from my earplugs. I could also feel it vibrate faintly through the tarmac apron our tents were set upon. The thought occurred to me that I could move the tent, but then I'd be nearer the BMW disco plane, which was thumping out some Balearic beats, with a Teutonic twist.

So, I rolled over in my sleeping bag and tried counting sheep…no they looked too much like goats. Bad idea.

But then the weirdness started, and it happened about two hours after I took my weekly Lariam anti-malaria tablet that evening. This was the 4th or 5th one, as I had begun the course back in the UK. The practice nurse had warned me there might be some side-effects from Lariam, but for some reason, they really kicked in that night in Atar.

Dreams began to surge in waves through my mind; cars, bikes and trucks roared in circles, people shouted at me in languages I had never heard before, the stars melted as if Van Gogh had painted them…all that good stuff.

Voices spoke to me, saying things I couldn't quite catch. Faces loomed close, whispering to me. Then I awoke in a blind panic. It felt like morning, an eerie light crept in my tent - yes, it was morning - shit, the flight!

I jumped out of my sleeping bag, heartbeat racing away, then packed my camera kit, notebook, water, sugary snacks etc. When I got out of the tent it was still dark. But hey, that was OK, I was just slightly early. Now, where was the Twin Otter again?

So, I strapped my torch to my head and set off to find the little yellow Otter aeroplane, tramping breathlessly past rows of sleeping people and the odd guard, standing around with his AK47 automatic and staring at me with great suspicion.

.

In reality, it was just gone one thirty in the morning, but inside my Lariam-fuzzed brain I was somehow convinced it was six am. I searched frantically for the right plane.

"Ca va?" asked a bemused guard as I wandered towards the bivouac.

"Oui, d'accord." I answered, staring at the parked aircraft, baffled that I couldn't see a yellow one amongst all the big, silver coloured fish, which were all now swimming in the sandy sea...and the wavy, gravy trees. Oh dear, my head hurts. I think I might be very, very sick in a minute.

I sat down for a while. I was so confused, I thought I was going to cry, or just start running away. Panic welled up in my guts and made me breathe rapidly. I had to talk to myself to argue over what was real, and what was imaginary. It was hard to say really. At one stage, a large rock turned into a lizard. Or it could have been the other way around. It was trippy, scary stuff.

Then I trudged back up the airfield. For some bizarre reason, which only made sense in my mind, I decided to wake up the Danish crew on our Press plane and get a seat inside, just to be ready in case we were leaving Africa. I knocked on the door and the pilot eventually answered;

"What's wrong?"

"I've missed the `plane to El Ghallaouiya, I need to get a seat here, otherwise I'll be stranded here forever." I jabbered. The pilot opened the cabin door and told me we were staying here for four days, plus he realised I was sleepwalking or some such nonsense, and then told me the correct time.

"Go to sleep, stop walking around like a damn fool."

"Right, OK, see you later. Sorry."

So I went back into my tent and slept for what seemed like ten minutes, then the alarm buzzed and I got up. Four hours had passed. Crazy.

Just feeling normal again was an incredible joy, a revelation. I packed my gear and easily made the Otter flight. Walking down the runway I gave the remaining strip of Lariam to a bored looking guard,

"Cadeaux M'sieur, enjoy! Bon chance."
"OK, merci, merci." He smiled broadly. Medication of any sort is always welcome in Africa. Better than dollars.

On the `plane I sat opposite an ugly, very aggressive, French lady journalist. She jabbered away nervously as we strapped in and the engine coughed into life. The Otter creaked as it taxied along. It felt like it was made of straw, wattle, daub and old bandages. I really didn't give a monkeys, I was utterly exhausted from a night that Keith Richards would have found mildly rock `n' roll.

Maybe it was a little trace of Lariam still in my system, but I considered opening the door and pushing her out as we chugged upwards into the sunrise sky.

"Madame, just shut the fuck up. I'm tired."

I spoke to nobody else on the flight, just stared out of the window. It had taken just a week to make me a Parisian.

When we landed, we went straight into little groups of three aboard a helicopter, which shuttled us to the rally camp itself at El Ghallaouiya.

This was the first time I had ridden in a helicopter and I loved it. It skimmed the surface of Mauritania with a fluid grace, dipping low near the orangey-brown trails in the land, driving smoothly upwards over the small peaks and then skirting the lip of a giant horseshoe of rock, inside which lay the rally bivouac.

It was one of the most unearthly sights of my life, and the most beautiful. A random cluster of people and machines lay below, there was bivouac smoke mixing with diesel fumes from a Kamaz truck, rising gently, as we glided effortlessly into camp. Everything seemed like flotsam and jetsam from a long forgotten shipwreck, the tents arranged in some odd formation, like a dyslexic signal for help.

We dropped, like litter, like angels, upon a slice of the world which looked like it had been slowly crushed, then sifted out the chaff of humanity.

****

Wide Eyed and Legless

Inside the bivvy, I am greeted by Neil, who looks shattered after volunteering to spend the night here, having been allowed up in the helicopters to do some pictures yesterday.

"I got coffee at six this morning," relates Neil, "then I started shaking so much from the cold I spilled most of it. It was f***ing freezing up here last night - and I had no sleeping bag."

"Shit, all your stuff's on the press plane." I realised.
"So long as it's still there...that's something."
"Nah, it is. They had the plane locked up most of yesterday and last night as well." I add, not telling Neil about my late night attempt to break into the Fokker.

I fished deep in my pocket and give Neil a chewy flapjack bar. Already I'd learned never to trust the TSO estimates on when food might arrive, or when food might be available at the next camp. So I squirrel away spare snack bars in my fisherman's gilet. Later in my life I'd discover I was pre-diabetic and needed regular food to stay mentally shipshape, but back on the Dakar I had sugar highs and lows, as well as the Lariam terrors. Back then, sudden mood swings seemed normal, just part of being on the rally.

We decide to rest in the shade for a while, as the heat at El Ghallaouiya was fearsome. This is the Sahara proper and apart from the surrounding arc of rock, there were dunes as far as you could see in the other direction. The heat seemed to rise by the minute. I could feel my flesh begin to burn, despite the layer of sun cream on my face and arms. It's only ten in the morning too. I realised that the afternoon would be utterly exhausting, we would need more water – and soon.

As the riders had pelted off on the 'yacht' stage, doing their GPS triangle, we waited for the lunchtime bivouac to be prepped up. There wasn't much else to do, as there was no press tent, just a basic TSO outpost with no really useful info and no way of emailing anything.

Suddenly, I have a mad idea; we could trek about two kilometres to the inflatable 'Dakar Rallye' arch, which marks the end of this stage. We can just see it in the distance, shimmering away in the heat haze. I suggest that we can take some 'typical' Dakar pics of the bikes passing under the 'Total Dakar Rallye' signage. Neil agrees this would be worth doing, so off we go.

Basically we were both a bit stir crazy by this time. It isn't easy being a prisoner of the French, let me tell you.

Nevertheless, with an extra bottle of water apiece, we trudge away, our feet sinking into the proper, Sahara-soft sand which fills this rock basin. The funny thing was that as we walked, the air seemed to get hotter with each breath that I took, until I felt like I was working in an industrial bakery. My legs felt heavier, my back was perspiring after just 100 metres or so. Under my bush hat, sweat dribbles from my hair into the edge of my eyes. At the halfway stage to the Dakar Rallye sign, Neil and I glance at each other and then give up.

"Shit. If we make it, we'll die before we shoot a roll of film." I say to Neil. Yep, we were still using transparency film in 2001. Neil nodded back at me and sat down.

We both drink half a litre of water, laugh at our own stupidity and then realise that one little sculptured fragment of this vast desert, these lapping waves of glass and dust, has utterly defeated us.

Lawrence of Arabia my arse.

****

About three hours later, the first bikes come in, and I do a quick interview with Deaks, who seems to have enjoyed the stage, even though it's a simple triangle route.

"It was OK out there today, made a few places up, so that's all we can do. Keep pluggin' away like." He says with typical understatement. I can imagine how oven-like it must be riding a motorcycle out there and dragging it out of deep sand-washes.

Neil packs his stuff up and we wait our turn for the brief helicopter ride to the airstrip and then back on the Twin Otter. There's the usual arguments with the French journos about stowing gear, much hand-waving and theatrical shrugging etc. but as the Otter's aircrew are German they brook no nonsense and immediately begin shouting at one journo;

"Pack this properly, or we are all dead – understand, ja?"

Some days I do love German bluntness. In many ways Germanic types are like taller Yorkshire people, but slightly more tolerant of vegetarians and nudists.

A short, giddy flight in the late afternoon sunshine and then we touch down again at Atar. Things are even more surreal, as we all watch an Air France 737 park up near the BMW Lear jet.

More VIPs? Nope, a charter excursion of Gap-wearing, Gaultier-fragrant, French adventurers has come to wallow in Atar's misery, just for one evening.

It felt distinctly odd to drag my weary bones, my sweat-soaked body, past immaculately dressed, clean people, as I carted all my kit back from the Twin Otter to my tent. Some of them took pictures of my sand-blasted, stubble-coated face, as I wandered past. Crikey, in just over a week I've become a local curiosity, a Dakar 'character.' Compo with a head torch.

Later, just after dark, they set up a full-on disco, plus bar, on the Tarmac next to the 737 and a small number of the tourists actually begin half-arsed attempts at dancing. The music continues thudding out until past one in the morning, which, as you can guess from my previous sleepless night on Lariam, wasn't that much fun for me. But then, imagine what it was like for the bedraggled rally riders themselves, many of whom had struggled to make it back to camp after completing two very long stages.

No rest. Just the sound of Sheila B. Devotion and Johnny Halliday booming out as you try to grab five hours sleep before the next 370-odd kilometres.

As I lay on my sleeping bag, earplugs ineffective against the bass thumping up from the ground, I also wondered what the locals made of it. This petrolhead circus, rolling through town with its beer tokens, mini-skirted PR girls and out-of-date pharmaceuticals.

You see, that's one way the Dakar rally literally dodges bullets; by donating old prescription drugs – lorry loads of them – to local politicians, as we traverse the Western Sahara.

Mostly, these were generic drugs, (generic means out of the seven year licence period, when pharma companies can charge a premium price to reclaim the research costs) just past their use-by date in Europe. So by donating them, the only real cost was transporting them to Atar. The drugs would simply have been destroyed otherwise.

Did all these aspirins, malaria treatments or antibiotics save lives? I couldn't really say, as I heard a rumour that after the photo opportunity was over, the lorry load of drugs donated at Atar was distributed to men in sunglasses driving Mercs and Toyota 4X4s.

Just a rumour, and I have to stress I didn't see local gangsters skimming off the lion's share of the pills, gels and liquids, but very little gets done in Africa without bribery and corruption playing a part in the process. Wheels have to be greased, even on the Dakar.

So maybe the people who needed the antibiotics couldn't afford them? It isn't corruption, it's just market forces?

Well, maybe so. After a while, you stop thinking about the morality of what you're doing out here in the desert. No single person can make a difference, except in the most tiny, almost pathetic way – you might buy someone's life for a day, maybe two, by giving them money. Or you might cost a child half his nose by dishing out free sweets. Fact is, your random act of kindness could go either way. Might even get you killed.

I tried to imagine life here in Mauritania without the cash cow Dakar rally blasting its high octane way through the nothingness. Like most locals, I would try and screw something, anything, out of this insane parade of technology, neo-colonialism and human endurance, as it rolled by. The alternative would be to lay down and wait for death in this slow cooking crematoria. No thanks.

Like so much in life, there's no simple black and white, good vs bad, answer to the questions that pop into your mind. You don't feel any better about it just lying in your tent feeling guilty either. Although you do have the urge to see certain jet-set tourists robbed at gunpoint obviously.

The Price of Water: How Bad Do You Want It?

In total, we spent four days in Atar. On the very first day, David Singer offered to let me use his portable shower – a black rubber bag hung on the wing of an aircraft, so long as I obtained the water for it.

This sounded like a sweet deal, as any shower in the Sahara feels like the luxurious gyrations of Kylie Minogue upon your skin. So, I took David's little water barrel on wheels and pushed it along the entire length of the airstrip to a low, greyish-white building right next to the Mauritanian air force hangar.

This hangar was fascinating because inside were two Hunter jets and a Dakota DC3. Yep, an absolutely mint DC3, pure time warp condition. Me and Alberto paid the guard about £2 each just to look at the thing but we weren't allowed to take photos of it. Beautiful sandy brown colour as well, pure Casablanca baby. Probably part of the Mauretanian El Presidente's classic aircraft collection.

On the first day, as we paid to see the plane, we got the water barrel filled for free. On the second, the price was two hundred Cfa – about £2.

But the guard realised he was onto a good thing having a water tap next to his AK47, so on the third day, the price went up to 400 Cfa. Still less than filling the barrel with litre bottles bought from the Dakar bivouac, but getting a bit cheeky. I tried to barter a pair of sweaty socks to get the price down, but no dice, this guy wanted cash.

On day four, you guessed it; the cost of filling the barrel was now 800 Cfa, which was taking the urine frankly. Must admit, I lost my marbles a bit and protested in the French style, with lots of arm-waving, `Merde!' type cursing and feeble attempts at haggling the price back down to 200.

In the end, the guard got tired of my mangled Franglais, made a `Whssst' noise and gestured at me to leave the area with the barrel of his gun.

I refused to back down too easily. As I was wearing sunglasses, I felt I could maintain a poker face, even if my bum was twitching a little bit.

"I take water for the aero." I informed him in bad French. "300 Cfa, s'il vouz plait…"

"Non, eight hundred." He said, in English this time, and holding the gun really close to my belly. Have to admit, I don't respond well to ultimatums.

"F*** you."

His sunglasses stared at my Foster Grants. Nobody moved. I figured that if he had ammunition for the AK47 then he would've probably sold it by now for ready cash.

"Whsst, allez. You f*** off." He said, pointing his AK straight at me. In the finest traditions of mad Brits in the sun, I removed my sunglasses, smiled sarcastically at him and then slowly, very slowly, dragged two hundred Cfa from my wallet.

I placed the cash under the ash tray on his little table and then went and turned the tap on. For a second I expected a rifle butt in the back of the head, but hey, he took the money. Then spat on the ground to show what he thought of me.

The following day was our final day at Atar and this time, he wouldn't sell me any water, at any price. In fact he seemed shocked that I had the brass cheek to even approach him with my water trolley on wheels. I must have had heatstroke, stupid thing to do.

"Wsshhht." He hissed again, dismissing me like he was swatting a fly. I muttered some swear words and once again got the pointy gun treatment. This time he removed his sunglasses and to be fair, he did have the cold, dead eyes of a killer that particular day, and so I thought better of my `place the cash on the table' ploy.

Maybe I just didn't feel so brave that day. Maybe I had better blood sugar levels. Whatever the case, I gave up on the tap. He could keep it. But I was still annoyed enough to stroll over to the edge of the runway, drop my shorts down and take a long, slow piss right in front of the empty desert, whilst showing my white butt at the victorious guard.

"Kiss my arse Tonto, I get to fly out of this shit hole tomorrow. You get to guard a tap all your frigging life."

Then I walked as casually as possible back, pushing the clattering little water barrel back to the `plane. Once there, I almost collapsed in fear, realising how completely stupid I was, risking my life over less than a tenner's worth of water.

"No water then?" observed Neil.
"Nah, that robbing soldier wanted 800 Cfa, just wasn't gonna pay it." I gave Neil the highlights of my Mexican stand-off. He looked baffled and rightly so, as I could easily afford the cost of the water, even if it had been 1600 Cfa. I think that Neil knew then that I was having some type of weird desert fever, mentalist breakdown.

"Oh well, shit happens. Let's go get a beer. Or three." He offered, as a temporary solution.

Which we did. In fact I got completely hammered and texted my wife even though the phone had no signal at all. Just felt I had to, because I needed to remind myself that I was still alive and still behaving like a complete pillock.

CHAPTER FIVE;

INTO THE EYE OF THE STORM

As we prepared to leave Atar, I began to feel a little better about the rally, thanks to the rest day we had there, plus packing in the Lariam tablets. My face fuzz was coming along nicely, which frightened off some other journos and rally personnel in general. This was good news in the food queues, or when squabbling over use of an electrical power point in the press tent.

Just to give you one small example of how petty it was, I plugged in the battery charging unit for the video camcorder, only to return to the tent some thirty minutes later to find someone had unplugged it to charge up their laptop.

So I re-connected my battery then sat with it, to prevent anyone else using it. It was the only way - other journalists pretended to write stuff, simply to keep their equipment charged up and working. It was a sad state of affairs, with threats issued now and then.

Lucky for me, very few journos now wanted to tackle a foul-smelling, facially hairy Brit, with a foreign legion type skinhead crop. Can't think why, as I'm crap at fighting and they easily outnumbered me.

There was one day of great excitement in Atar, as Roma fell off and badly damaged his leg, a few kilometres from the end of the stage, which effectively ended his race there and then.

When he was helicoptered into Atar, a French journalist - who had previously refused to speak any English to me, suddenly said;

"Is your camera digital?"
"No, it's got slide film in."
"Your video, is that digital? I need a shot of Roma - quickly, he arrives now!"
"You can hire some video for cash, say £250?" I said, seeing an opportunity to profit from the moment.

"What? F*** you." Was the response from the French journo, who seemed to have magically discovered the ability to converse in English under pressure.

"F*** you too, buy your own camera. Don't forget the battery charger cable either." I replied, wandering outside to try and get a shot myself as the medivac chopper blew dustclouds in our faces as it landed.

But Roma was surrounded by a pack of French TV media, one of whom elbowed me in the face as I tried to get a photo or two. I leaned my camera over his head and fired off a few random shots, then bashed the camera on his head as he was filming.

Well, I figured to myself, if this motorcycle journo thing doesn't work out, I could always try a career as an international diplomat.

****

Early, very early, as light began to haze colour into the sky, I waited with my camera gear, next to the media helicopters.

This was the one day that I was to be allowed on the press chopper, which followed the rally leaders all along the route, in tandem with the French TV `copter. Naturally, everyone else on the chopper was French, so three of us journo/photographers squeezed in, along with the pilot. I said good morning and some shit about who I worked for in French, but only got a grunted reply from anyone on board. Oh well.

The helicopter ride itself however, was superb; a truly unforgettable day, which was one of the highlights of the entire event.

The route that day was pretty straightforward, but crossed some 500 kilometres of serious, strength-sapping desert between Atar and the capital city of Mauritania, Nouakchott, located on the coast.

The previous front runners, Joan Roma and France's Richard Sainct were now out of the rally (Sainct's bike expired on the way to Atar, just before Roma crashed out) so the French press were now mainly interested in the car section, where the famously argumentative Jean-Marie Schlesser was in with a chance of victory, driving a very trick Renault dune buggy. It sounded like a Porsche GT racer, looked like a semi-squashed blue beetle and had the four wheel traction of a Range Rover.

But as the bikes always start the day's stage first, we flew ahead for maybe 15-20 minutes, and then set down in a village, so we could get pics of the leading bikes racing along the Sahara tracks.

Once the turbo whine of the helicopter had whistled away, as the engine shut down, the near silence was eerie, with just bleating goats and the odd chanting of `Cadeaux M'sieur' from the villagers, who had emerged from their huts, happy that some European money had literally dropped from the sky that day.

The 'houses' that they lived in were a handful of tiny, round, clay blockhouses. One or two had a kind of roof, to block out the sun, but others had assembled leaves, bits of sacking and dry, cracked wood, to fashion a shelter, maybe eight to ten feet in diameter. These were family homes.

It looked a miserable, gnawing fight to exist in this scorched, near barren piece of land. I wondered why they stuck it out, but then guessed that they were from the wrong tribe to survive ten minutes in say Nouakchott. Your tribe was everything here in the desert, because so much around you was full of nothingness. You had to be part of something bigger to survive.

The bikes droned in the distance, and then suddenly breezed past, skimming the surface of the earth like a barber's electric clippers sculpting new lines of hair. The burly, imposing figure of Fabrizio Meoni looked smooth, physically dominating his sliding KTM like an alpine skier. Then came Alfie Cox, Sala, de Garvado and others passing effortlessly by, riding relaxed, and conserving energy.

By contrast, they were followed by Jimmy Lewis and Cyril Despres, really hacking their BMWs through the soft sandy trail. Almost wrestling the big 900 twins, as if they were encouraging reluctant carthorses into some medieval battle. I admired Lewis for keeping up with the leading KTMs, on what was obviously a difficult bike to ride, mainly because BMW were persevering with the idea that a big Boxer twin could win a race which was so obviously an ideal event for a lightweight, single cylinder bike. Sheer power was little use out here.

Then the chopper's engine whirled up and we were summoned back for another breathtaking fly-ride, this time tracking the cars.

So we skimmed around in a big arc, seeing motorcycle

riders shooting beneath and beside us as they hammered along the harder sections of sand, at 80 -100mph, with the two French snappers hogging the open side door, getting some shots, as we flew about 60 feet above the ground.

They forced me to sit upfront in the `copter's boiling hot plastic bubble, alongside the pilot. But I was lucky, because my video camcorder got some decent footage of Schlesser almost hitting camels as he bounced and slewed along the tracks.

At one point, Schlesser realised he was lost, stopped the car completely, and then forked off at a sixty degree angle, almost wiping out a steady, almost touring motorcycle rider, as he charged back up the field. You might not have liked the guy, but there was no denying his will to win. He was on the edge of a big fight all the time, mainly with himself.

We stopped once more, to drop off the most arrogant of the two French photographers on board, who decided he would hitch a lift with a support vehicle for the last 50 kilometres or so. Good riddance to deeply annoying rubbish, plus there was more room inside the tiny helicopter.

As we buzzed some 300 feet above the competitors, then encountered actual Tarmac roads as we neared Nouakchott, I reflected on what I'd seen out in the `true' desert today.

The bleakness, the lack of any waypoints like mountains, trees or buildings was unnerving. It was an enormous cradle of heat and dust; the ashes of dead empires, lost slave caravans, and defeated armies lay around you. Silent, buried deep and watching, unblinking as time. This desert was patiently, relentlessly expanding, drawing nearer to Nouakchott, dune by marching dune. Raw, uncompromising nature will take us all, one day.

It was the closest that I came to seeing the race through the competitors eyes, as the Sahara unfurled its grit and rippling dunes before us, seemingly endless, in every direction. I understood now why so many Spanish speaking racers and drivers entered this event; it was pure Cervantes, completely Quixotic. A pointless, high speed tilt at danger, yet life-enhancing for all that; a beautiful challenge against your own mortality.

The bikes wriggled and squirmed as the riders bounced across rocks, or gunned their machines through soft `washes' of fine white sand. From 60 feet above, it was like watching a pack of 100mph surfers. They were as graceful as cats sometimes and then awkward, ungainly, as they suddenly scrabbled for grip, desperately trying to recover from a near accident. I just couldn't believe that they rode so damn fast, all the time, on the edge of their ability.

Don't ever underestimate what it takes just to finish a race like the Dakar. This event will find you out, punish you, mock your moments of mental weakness and poor planning. The desert will expose your glass jaw and lamp you one.

****

We traced a huge arc in the sky, taking a last look at the cars, before touching down once again, this time near a wadi, where stunted bushes and trees signalled the elusive presence of moisture somewhere beneath the earth.

The helicopter's blades had just stopped turning when a tribesman appeared from behind a bush. He was gaunt, with a hard, lined face that peered at me like the alien I was to him. tall, Dressed in the blue robes of the Tuareg, he had a certain authority that was intimidating. They were slavers for centuries and you can still see that steely will, that coldness in their eyes.

He nodded at me, but in a cursory way and then asked for a gift. I shrugged 'Non' and he merely stood and watched, eyes glinting, as I took a series of pictures of the riders going by, and a few cars, all ploughing their own furrows through the soft trail.

I drank about half of my second bottle of water. I would have finished it, but the sudden whine of the helicopter whining into life gave me a hurry-up signal. I offered him the water and said 'Cadeaux, bon chance.'

He took it and gave me another nod, this time with more inflection. As I walked away, I threw a sugary cereal bar at the Tuareg man, breaking the promise I had made to myself that I wouldn't dish out charity like tips in a cheap restaurant. But the place was desolate, beautiful, unearthly and I was somehow impressed that he asked once for a 'cadeaux' then said nothing else. He might beg, but only the once.

Again, he just nodded. Think he preferred to enslave others, rather than take a white man's charity. But today was an exception. There's one for Radio 4's Moral Maze programme eh?

To this day, I don't know if that snack bar made a shred of difference to his chances of survival, and yet I still did it.

Like *Live Aid*, or giving old clothes to Oxfam, all it does is salve a trace of guilt that you feel, as one lucky human gazes for a harsh second or two into the eyes of someone less fortunate, someone without the luxury of choice. Because that's all morality is when you boil it right down to unpleasant, basic facts of life – a luxury that is granted to us by our full bellies in the West.

The only real significance of the gesture, the only saving grace, is that both sides acknowledge the simple yet profound cruelty of life's lottery, and the unlikelihood of it ever changing. For there is no God, nor conscience, but what we make.

****

On the run in to Nouakchott, we catch Schlesser once more. As he charges over hills and dunes at 60 -120mph, he narrowly misses another slow biker, driving recklessly again.

To me, Schlesser is the fiery heart of this French faux-colonial adventure, this last gasp jaunt across their post-Suez empire.

He drives full speed, like a Gallic Mr Toad, and to hell with anything in his way. Like a deranged Musketeer, high on expensive sugar-coated pastries and coffee that could strip varnish at Versailles, Schlesser rampages onwards. All he cares about is winning, for the glory of France, the thrill of the sport, blah-blah-blah. Schlesser is part of that faintly repulsive hardcore of French people on the Dakar, who regard the Sahara as their own giant sandpit, a playpen for them and their magnificent machines.

Orwell once wrote that to know imperialism, you had to be part of it. In that helicopter, understanding fragments of the racist conversation crackling into my earphones, or dishing out snack foods in the sand, I felt dressed in the last, shabby coat-tails of empire. For all the personal courage of the competitors, and many others on the event, this race was still a little too `foreign legion' at times.

Finally, we could make out a haze ahead. Then it became light blue, with an immense, broken teeth scattering of white houses clustered on the edge of the brilliant Atlantic Ocean. This was Nouakchott, the fish gutting capital of the Western Sahara.

I could smell the fish and the salt as soon as we landed. It was everywhere and I swear the chicken sandwich I wolfed down in the bivvy tent tasted kinda fishy. After filling up on food and a swift beer, I walked towards the press tent, which was near the edge of this busy airport, right next to the main terminal.

People milled about, some TSO, some journos, some local hustlers and taxi drivers. Many of the French were negotiating the cost of a night in a local hotel, but I didn't fancy it, especially on my own – it was too risky. But I wandered out of the gate and had a look down the street which led towards the city centre.

I spoke with a local taxi man who twigged I was English within seconds.

"Hey, non Francais…English yes? Manchester United, Arsenal…I love England man. Where do you want to go? Let's go to a nice place, plenty of girls, cheap beers too."

"Nah, d'accord. It's OK, I'm married."

The taxi man looked me up and down, just in case I seemed gay and he could sell me some young boys instead. Then he complimented me on my beard, but asked;

"You want shave? You need razor blades or electric, there is Boots the Chemist in town. I will take you, yes?"

For some reason this made me laugh out loud. I pictured it; Boots the Chemist, in Mauritania's answer to Grimsby, with those annoying white-coated women trying to sell Clinique potions, or asking if you had your loyalty card. The craziness of it made me rock with laughter. I was back in civilization, I could just step off this mental circus, and escape back to reality.

But no, instead I turned around thanked the taxi man, and went back behind the barrier to join the other lunatics.

I picked up my tent and gear from photographer Neil, who had looked after it whilst I was on the chopper for the day. This was essential practice, as a Russian journalist had discovered a few days earlier. All his clothing, used films, notebooks, food etc. had mysteriously disappeared, whilst he had foolishly left his stuff inside his tent for the day.

The typically bear-like Russian journo shouted and ranted at Marie-Christine, who was in charge of media operations, but she - with her usual Gallic indifference - assured him this was nothing to do with her, and secondly, the bags would turn up eventually.

She then suggested he borrow some stuff from his `journalist friends.'

Oh really? These would be the same `friends' who were almost physically fighting over plug sockets in the Press Tent every night eh? Yeah right.

Nouakchott was a good stopover however, for one supreme reason. There was a toilet block which we foreign scum journos were allowed to use – for free - in the airport terminal buildings. I watched carefully as one or two other people walked in and out, past the guard nearby. No money changed hands - remarkable. Amazing.

Didn't these guards know this was Africa, were they new in town? They were letting people use a facility for free, the crazy fools.

However, after using this revolting `hole-in-the-ground' toilet, and opting for my own loo paper, rather than the small bucket of rancid water next to the wall, I was delighted to discover a faint trickle of water from the wash basin. They have running water here too. Wow. I risked a little splash of it on my face to clear the sand and dirt away, being careful not to swallow any, or let it get into my nostrils. There was a cracked, dirty mirror in the loo as well, and I saw my own reflection for the first time in over two weeks. I was afraid, very afraid. I looked like a tramp who had passed out in a tanning salon, after a heavy night on the meths.

"Oh you ugly werewolf, grrrrr." I said, just as someone vaguely Mediterranean walked in behind me. The guy shot me a glance, and then averted his eyes. For the first time in my dull life, I was capable of intimidating people. Although it was only the descent into mild insanity that was scaring people away. Letting yourself go to rack and ruin and taking mind-altering malaria treatments can do that. You basically appear to have nothing left to lose, and that always scares people.

I tested my endurance after a wash n brush up, by hiking over a kilometre in blazing late afternoon heat back to the bivouac. Rally personnel and pit crew blew up small sandstorms as they passed me on quads and scooters. Nobody gave me a lift as I was plainly British, and some kind of half-man, half-Airedale terrier.

When I got to the tented canteen area, I bought some water, a beer, plus some snacky food - the evening meal wasn't quite ready yet, and then dusted myself down in the shade, next to some French blokes. My feet were hurting again after the hike, so I took off my desert hiking boots.

One of the Frenchies nearby asked me to put them back on. In French of course.

I just shrugged, as if I didn't understand a word. So he did an international mime, pulling invisible boots onto his feet, tying up laces, then holding his nose and pulling a comedy face of disgust.

I responded by pointing slowly at him, and then inserted my finger inside a hole I made with my thumb and forefinger, and then vigorously moved the finger back and forth in the hole.

"F*** you." Frankly, after a day in a tiny helicopter cockpit with the world's rudest photographer prick, I really was ready to nut someone.

There was a rapid discussion amongst the French trio, which included a few choice swear words, but although there were three of them, nobody wanted to start on me. They just weren't sure if I was perhaps so hungry that I would eat great chunks of their faces.

"You Anglais, football scum." said one of them, as they decided to pack up and have their picnic at a table located near the other end of the tent.

"Catch you later Marshal Petain. Enjoy the Vichy side of the tent."

Ah yes, the benefits of a history degree.

****

On the way back from the bivouac photographer Neil and I spotted a really old looking aircraft parked up and getting loaded with fish. It was an Antonov 12 B I think – I'm no plane spotter – but it definitely had four propeller engines, a creaking Cold War style fuselage and what appeared to be gun turrets front and back. No really, the guns had gone but the turrets were there.

Neil took a few photos and the Russian crew waved and said hello to us.

"Hey, you want a lift home – we take you to London for $1000 each!" they joked; at least I think they were joking. Russian pilots in 2001 were all mercenaries, as the 1990s had seen the collapse of the Soviet Union and everything seemed to be for sale as the 21st century dawned.

We got closer and watched the local guys manhandling pallet loads of stuff, along with refrigerated boxes crammed with stinky fish. One of the aircrew stepped down and shook our hands.

"Hey come inside, see the plane yes? Five dollars each, we give you the tour."

So we gave the pilot the Cfa equivalent of five bucks and clambered inside the belly of the beast. It was amazing. Wires and cables were everywhere, taped together, bolted, welded, bodged in every way you could imagine.

The rear turret had a kind of jump seat in there, plus a Bakelite radio set, some mysterious instruments (why would you need them at the back of the plane?) and heavy steel boxes that looked like ammo boxes, but were probably stuffed full of drugs and porn.

The cockpit was equally Dr Strangelove, with tons of old school dials and pointy arrows, red switches marked with Russian script and a couple of cramped seats behind the pilot and co-pilots chairs. It really was a vintage machine, you could not believe that any commercial air cargo company was still using a shitty old crate like this.

We declined the pilots' kind offer of a lift to Murmansk, or wherever the hell they were off to, and thanked them for the guided tour. They began their pre-flight checks as we squeezed past cargo and back down the aluminium ladder.

We sat down about 200 metres away and finished our beers off as the Antonov gradgrinded its way into life. First one smoky barbeque engine, then another chimed in – reluctant as an England player taking penalties against Germany – before the last two motors spat soot, neat fuel and probably fish guts out and then began whirring away. Soon the noise was deafening and we moved another 100 metres or so down the runway.

As the sun set, the Antonov graunched its saggy undercarriage left and right, shook its weary flaps, like some tired, rime-spattered albatross, and revved its prop turbos for all it was worth, shaking the very ground next to us. Smoke belched out, in an almost Victorian cotton mill way, as the pilot freed the brakes and let her go down the runway. At what appeared to be walking pace.

"Jeeeeesus, it's never going to take-off, it must be massively overloaded." observed Neil, as he snapped his last shots in the gathering gloom. The vapour trails poured out of the engines as the plane bellowed like a dying walrus. Then finally, at the last possible second, the 12 B groaned mournfully into the air, exhaling the stench of Africa, like a flock of black crows gathering in the sky.

"Now that's flying." I said.

"That's Russian Roulette." replied Neil.

****

During the night at Nouakchott, there is a small collision between one of the rally planes and a commercial airliner, at about two in the morning. Space is tight because there are 15-ish planes on the rally, plus Air France, and other airlines, run regular services to Nouakchott. There is much shouting, revving of engines etc. and basically everyone in the camp has to wake up as aircraft taxi about and spotlights are fired up to inspect the damage.

A Russian Antonov jet has a neat little dent in its fuselage, where a wing tip has thumped into it. Oh well, shit happens, nobody died. I go back to sleep about 4am.

After daybreak, I get up and learn that our press plane is about number five or six on the flight plan, which means we have about an hour to kill, having packed all our gear up and foraged for breakfast tea or coffee.

Unlike others, I don't make a dash to the bivouac for breakfast, as I have learned to stash away as much food as possible the night before. You have to wrap it ultra-carefully to avoid insects attacking it, but it can be done.

So, I watch the French TV Herc take off, and then it is the turn of the damaged Antonov, despite the protests of the French medical team, who are flying on a plane which has a neat little plate welded over a fresh crack in its fuselage. Some of the team don't want to get on the plane and start arguing with rally control.

It is so funny watching the French falling out with each other for a change. After ten minutes delay they are told to get on, or walk home. Sheepishly, they get on. I wave at them cheerfully as the Antonov revs its fearsomely crude engines.

"Byeee - bon voyage mes amis!" I shout over to them. Nobody answers.

But of course, it is alright. The plane is flying at low altitude anyway, but nothing leaks, the plate stays welded on and they make it without problems to Tidjika, which is the next stop on the rally.

****

When it's our turn to fly, we take off smoothly, but soon encounter some choppy winds and have to fly fairly high to avoid a couple of sandstorms. The captain warns us that there is a big sandstorm at Tidjika, but mentions it in that calm, reassuring voice pilots use.

As the Fokker circles towards the landing strip, I can just make out a fuzzy outline of the town below. An orange-brown fog swirls below us, and then the plane begins to creak and shake its wings as we enter the storm itself. There is a bump, and I'm jolted out of my seat, as the Fokker's engines cough and we hit a pocket of dead air. It is eerie when there is no lift beneath the wings for a second or two.

People around me start to look concerned. I can see nothing out of the window, then a glimpse of desert…no wait, it's gone again. This is drama. The stewardess Gida looks like her smile is painted on as she sits facing us behind the cockpit.

Chris Evans, the English-French translator on the Dakar shouts cheerfully;

"We're all going to die – text your wives…and girlfriends!" as the Fokker drops in another ghostly space of still, unsupportive air.

As I gaze down out from my window seat, I realise at about 500 feet that I can see the runway ahead, and it's to the right of us. If I can see it, then we're obviously some distance to the left of it…which means we're going to land in Tidjika High Street, or a big old patch of sand. Hmmm, that might not be good either way.

Suddenly the pilot gives it full throttle, and the entire plane shakes its rivets loose as we start to climb upwards again, battling the evil crosswind. After a steeply banked turn and another teeth-rattling descent through the eye of the storm, we touchdown with a heavy thump onto the gravel airstrip, swerve a little bit under braking, then park up carefully.

"Jesus f***ing Christ." says Neil next to me.
"Yep, we earned a beer today." I agree, sweating profusely. That was close. That was one fugly landing. But then, our day got worse. We stepped off the plane into that same sandstorm and the bitch just wanted to shred our eyes, ears, nostrils, lungs and arse cracks, all at the same time.

It's hard to describe how dispiriting a sandstorm is, unless you have suffered the scratchy, blinding and powerless humiliation of trying to function in one for a few hours. At first, the sand whipping like little glass needles past our arms and legs was an exciting novelty - a real taste of the Sahara.

Then Neil and I watched a couple of planes land perilously close to the Fokker and decided it was safer to make for the bivouac, even though pitching a tent was totally impossible in this wind. To make life harder, we were carrying German journo, Peter Mayer's bag with us. Because Peter was German he was very organised, which meant his bag contained about 70 kilos of equipment.

That trek along the airstrip, then across to the sand strewn, half-collapsed bivvy tents, was perhaps just one mile or so. Yet it must have taken us over an hour to make it, stopping for six rests on the way. Sand filled my fingernails, eyes and hair, my neck was gently grazed and blooded by one invisible flick knife of high speed glass. Hell, even my underpants gained weight – and not in a good way. You simply gave up trying to talk, so much sand got into your throat you felt yourself begin to choke. You couldn't spit it out quickly enough as you tried to trek onwards. It was grim. The locals stood by, swaddled in robes and no doubt pissing themselves laughing at us walking about in this hellish weather episode.

When we arrived at the bivouac, there was no catering truck, just a couple of empty marquee type tents, plus a few team trucks parked up and getting embedded by piles of sand gathering around their wheels. Naturally, nobody in Nouakchott had told us that there would be no lunch in Tidjika and that we should grab a packed lunch at breakfast. Luckily, I still had some stored food and water on me.

Neil and I shared two chocolate bars, a pack of two biscuits, like you get in a hotel minibar and a litre of water at lunchtime. That was all I had.

The wind carried on. Sand blew in under the tent folds. It was obvious we would need more water to last until seven at night, which was when the evening meal was usually ready. By this time a few other hungry journos had joined us sheltering from the sand blizzard outside. A French-Canadian girl called Anne-Marie volunteered to go foraging for us. We agreed that as she spoke French very well, and being female, she might elicit more pity than some hairy-arsed bloke journos.

She scrounged around the team trucks parked behind us and bagged a few litres of water, plus a couple of food ration packs as well - top girl!

In the heat of that long day, I'm certain that some of us would have simply passed out otherwise - water never tasted so good, so exhilarating, as it did in that six hour sandstorm. The howling Sahara was a bitch that day and I never want to feel that helpless, so imprisoned by nature, ever again.

****

The storm continued to blow until late afternoon, by which time, Neil and I had agreed there was no point in even trying to set up our tents, so we made a kind of mini camp inside one of the bivouac marquees.

This was a good plan, until the riders arrived, got fed at night, and then proceeded to crawl into their sleeping bags alongside us - the stench of sweat, petrol (one idiot cleaned his carbs right behind us, even though others were smoking) beery farts etc. wasn't too bad. But the noise from a couple of dozen snoring, exhausted enduro racers, was unreal. Even with earplugs in, I think I got about two hours sleep.

Next day was quieter, plus you could see the blue of the sky, which was nice. In fact, it was heaven.

But the day descended into farce for many of the privateer bikers, as they suddenly found themselves victims of another cunning French plan to get them off the rally.

The rally rules state that riders can miss up to eight Control Points (CPs) on the stages overall, but they must make the start and finish the day's stage. Talking later that morning with Mike Hughes, he told me that a group of privateers agreed to go out to CP1, get their card stamped, then return - basically treating today as an extra rest day.

Suddenly rally control issues a statement saying about a dozen riders may be `disqualified for not trying hard enough.'

I attend the riders meeting later that day, where an official reluctantly agrees to `clarify the rules' and a compromise is reached; no disqualifications, but 11 hour time penalties instead. Mike Hughes is visibly relieved;

"I can't believe the Dakar officials - they just make stuff up as they go along. They were going to boot us off for following their flaming rules, to the letter. I think they're starting to panic that too many bikes are going to arrive in Dakar - I reckon they haven't got enough space booked to ship the vehicles back to France, so they're hoping to bin off a few dozen of us. Devious, very devious."

****

As the wind dies down, so the leading riders arrive from the long day's loop in the desert. John Deacon has made a hard charge today, trying to claw back time, but finished 9th on the stage today, after falling off at speed and banging himself up. You can see his face swelling as he carefully removes his helmet.

"I was trying not to go too crazy," says Deaks, as he removes his riding gear, "but then I went off big time and the bike landed on top of me. Bad news, especially as the engine was still running and I couldn't reach the kill switch for a while. It damaged the oil cooler, but I managed to re-route the oil around it and make it back here - don't think there's much oil left in that motor though."

It wasn't until Deaks removed his body armour and trail pants, that I realised how hard he had landed. He moved slowly, awkwardly, grimacing as he squeezed his battered body inside his tent. Already, a large red mark signalled the start of massive bruising on his leg. He had been lucky out there, very lucky.

Absolutely nobody in the BMW pit crew offered Deaks any food or water. To be fair, they had a bike to fix, as quickly as possible, but even so, I felt there was a distinct bias towards Despres and Andrea Mayer in the team. Deaks and Lewis were left to fend for themselves as far as I could see.

The more I got know John Deacon, the more I admired his courage and laid back determination. He always had time to chat with people and he stayed cheerful, no matter what happened during the race, or behind the scenes in the pits. Psychologically, he seemed the strongest rider in the BMW team at that point. By this stage I was used to BMW's `help yourself' approach to their riders' thirst, so I gave Deaks a bottle of water that I'd blagged in advance from the bivouac earlier.

"Ah, cheers buddy, nice one."

Despres, by contrast, rarely spoke and tended to do lots of Gallic scowling. Meanwhile Jimmy Lewis was digging deep inside his soul to combat the pain from his wrists. Mostly, Jimmy looked shattered emotionally and physically after each stage. He wore a cowboy hat sometimes when off the bike, and I felt that for him the race was an extended rodeo – he was fighting with the BMW machine. Constantly battling.

Andrea Mayer seemed content to hold steady in midfield, hoping that the few other female racers in the event would break down, or crash out, thus giving her victory in the women's class. I couldn't fault her strategy as there were just two lady riders left ahead of her by that point I think – although forgive my faulty memory if I'm wrong.

The Dakar is an incredibly hard event for women. Although in some ways Mayer had it slightly easier as she rode the F650 single, not the big, lairy 900 twin. In other ways she had more psychological pressure. Women had no separate toilets, or sometimes, there were no toilets at all.

Now before you think `so what?' consider what it's like to be female and expose yourself to Muslim men who think that women should be at home, wearing a black robe and looking after children. Not racing bikes. Some of the men are armed with guns and feel that white European women are `fair game' as well.

Mayer also survived an attack by local thieves on one stage. She stopped to make adjustments to the BMW in a village, and was surrounded by young men. Once they realised she was a woman, they tried to steal her bike, then clothing and anything else they could think of - it could have been very nasty. But a rally helicopter appeared overhead and the locals ran away.

Andrea laughed off the incident as being `one of those things, there are good people and bad people everywhere' and that impressed me. She had more courage than many of the male competitors in the bike class. She was strong enough to lift her bike out of a dune when she crashed, but she was also capable of enduring almost anything this event threw at her. In her mind, she already visualised the finish line and saw herself crossing it.

There was no self-doubt in her head and that is a rare thing in motorcycle racing.

****

Next morning we packed up early, grabbed breakfast, plus a ration pack, as we knew our next stop was Tichit, allegedly one of the most beautiful places on the rally.
As we buckle up our seatbelts in the Fokker, Gida, the Danish stewardess informs us over the tannoy; "Well that was a pleasant stay in Tidjika, but now we are going to a place which is called shit, but I believe is quite alright really, so fasten your belts and let's get ready to rock and roll."

There's a sudden lifting of the mood on the plane. Nearly everybody feels utterly drained by the two days of sand blowing into our faces at Tidjika, so it's great to look forward to the moment of escape from this fly-blown hellhole.

However, touchdown some 30 minutes later in Tichit reveals…yet more sand blowing around our sunburnt knees.

Neil and I watch the Japanese journos try and erect their tents near the Fokker, as the wind blasts its hot breath around us. They remain steadfast, despite the wind blowing some of their kit away as they struggle to hold down guy ropes, bang in pegs and use several large stones to anchor down their nylon homes.

Then they crawl inside. Neil and I look at each other and nod. We don't speak; we don't want a mouthful of sand. I point towards the bivouac tent, which is semi-collapsed, just like the one at Tidjeka. You can see lumps moving, as people crawl under the marquee's heavy folds.

Chris Evans has an ingenious solution to camping out in sandstorms; crawl underneath the canvas and prop up your luggage to make a mini tent pole. It works, in a weird, claustrophobic, almost coal miner type of way. Soon, there are a couple of dozen people huddled under the giant awning, all holding conversations in different languages and barely visible behind stacked rucksacks and camera cases, even though we are just a few feet away from them. Very odd.

Near lunchtime, the catering crew make an attempt to pull the main tents up on the poles and weigh them down securely. So we get chucked out. Chris Evans wanders off with a French woman he knows, to have a look at the old town. The woman has spent the last year living here and has bought land, intending to make some kind of life for herself in her middle/old age.

I try to figure out why; no medical care, a dirt airstrip, dodgy water, plus a town full of hungry people ruled by men with two foot long sticks - who are pretty keen to use them on anyone stepping out of line. It's hard to see the attraction, apart from the sheer remoteness from any trace of civilisation. I wonder what demons in her past she's trying to escape. Tichit feels like the end of the earth, a blasted heath where human ashes are scattered.

The tent raising attempt fails, as the wind is too strong. We try to crawl under again but we are told to piss off anyway. S'il vouz plait.

We trudge across the sand again and pitch our tents in the leeward side of the small cluster of canvas, already sheltering near the Fokker's fuselage. I manage to flake out for an hour or so, feeling utterly exhausted as the temperature is now somewhere around 100 Fahrenheit. When I awake, the bikes are arriving, earlier than expected.

The BMW riders sprawl in the sun. They have beaten their back-up truck, so they have no shade, no tents. Not even any water. I pass a half litre bottle to Deaks and we lean against the wheel of another team's Jeep, chit-chatting as Deaks winds down from finishing second on today's stage;

"Thought I had the win today, but I miscounted the KTM boys - bloody Tainan shot off again into the distance. Sod it. Got some time back anyway." says JD, who is now running 6th overall.

"Cyril looks fed up." I observe, watching Despres mooch about, chatting with the German press officer.

"Cyril's my back-up, the water boy really, but he doesn't like it. Nobody does, but this is only his second time on the Dakar, so the chances of him getting a top three are remote. Thing is, he's a bit younger than me, he'll have his turn, but you know...he's French. He thinks he should win. So do the organisers most likely…"

"Yeah, I know what you're saying." I agreed. The fact was that the BMW factory effort had Gauloises cigarettes as the main sponsor - a financial twist not lost on Despres, who was keen to make an impression with the French media, by putting one over the `Rosbif' if he could. But Despres was simply too far back at this stage to persuade BMW team manager, Bertie Hauser, to give him the green light to attack the latter stages.

As in all motorsport, there's always more to it than just pure talent, or luck. Politics and money are always at work behind the scenes.

"You still reckon that the KTMs are gonna expire then John?" I enquired.

"One or two of `em, for sure. There's no way all five of them are going to bomb along quite happily all the way to the line. Thing is with the Dakar, it's got the faster stages at the end, which suits the big BMW twin better, plus there's all sorts of hazards ahead; bloody mad monkeys, thorn bushes that puncture your tyres, massive sinkholes in the road, more f***ers with guns - all sorts of shit to come yet.

"Bloody hell. Glad I'm taking the plane."

Deaks gave me a wry smile, then added; "One more thing, It gets hotter yet boy!"

"Really?"

"F*** me yes, proper sweaty back Africa hot. Humid, really saps at you. Means you can get dehydrated quick, and drink your camel pack too fast. As you get into the stage then you get giddy as you sweat all the water out of your body. You make a mistake. Game over."

"Tell me something, do you guys ever stop for a piss on the race stages?" I ask naively. Only someone who has never competed in any enduro races could ask that.

"Nah, mostly you sweat all the liquid out, otherwise just piss down one leg when you're riding a flat section. Or both legs...if you're Andrea." winked the big fella.

Later on, as the sun and the wind died away, the mountains that framed Tichit in a giant horseshoe of rock turned orangey-brown, the music blared from the French TV screen, set up in the bivouac and the cold beers tasted so sweet. This place did possess a strange, other worldly beauty, a raw slice of scenery rising from an immense plain surrounding it. I could see that in some ways, it was a type of fortress against the modern world; it had a raw simplicity that you could admire.

Still have to pay me to live there though.

****

The saddest memory I have of Tichit is the way we left it.

In the morning the aircraft crews carefully peeled away the engine covers, cleaned out sand where they could see it, made their checks and fired up in sequence. Everything worked, which was a tiny miracle. Our next stop was Nema in the South of Mauritania and our press plane was near the back of the queue in today's flight plan.

I watched the helicopters arc away into the sky first, as we ate breakfast in the bivouac. The riders and drivers had long since left, as there was a dawn start for them and the stage start line was a few miles down the trail.

So we were amongst the last to be eating, as the catering crew began packing up. There was a slightly tense atmosphere as various locals flitted about the bivvy, scratching around in the sand near our feet for scraps of food and litter, as the catering crew packed black liners with rubbish. After grabbing some packed lunches for later in the day, we trudged away back across the sand towards the planes. More locals watched us with hungry eyes.

Team trucks began to move out, couple of press cars too. In the distance, the massive Hercules roared down the gravel airstrip, raising huge swirls of sand in its wake. The mountains shimmered in the rising heat, the people from the town gathered near the ropes which marked the boundaries of our camp. Pained, drawn faces looked at us, staring, occasionally shouting a few words in French at us. Begging, always begging.

In their shoes, or rather no shoes, I'd do the same. Why should these rich white bastards stay one night and leave us nothing except a van load of expired flu vaccines?

I packed up, helped with the baggage loading on the Fokker, just for something to do, whilst several of the French journalists skived off somewhere else, or simply stood chatting nearby, totally ignoring the work which was being done in front of them.

By this stage, I was oblivious to their general laziness, my only concern was enduring the event without punching someone.

There were perhaps just two or three planes left as our Fokker revved up and we started to taxi towards the little quad bike, which was parked at the end of the runway. The guy on the quad bike was air traffic control here, that's how it worked – if he said fly, off you went.

The runway was clear, so our engines growled and we began to leave Tichit. I stared out of the window and saw some of the locals make a break from behind the ropes, trying to catch the few bags of rubbish which danced around on the sand in the wake of our propellers.

A couple of town elders, or local mafia - whatever you want to call them - armed with long, thin sticks, and began to beat the backs and heads of those who crossed the rope barrier. They then kicked a few of the persistent litter scavengers. For the sake of a Coke can, a child received a savage whack across the head, which knocked him flat onto his little belly, hands covering his head, as he scrambled away in the swirling sand.

I turned away and looked down at the interior of the plane. I didn't want to see anymore of Tichit. There wasn't a damn thing any of us could do, but leave them to it.

****

CHAPTER SIX;

LIFE'S LITTLE ESCAPE ROUTES

Nema was a border way post, set on the so-called 'Road of Hope' which ran south into Mali. Some hope, Mali is one of the poorest countries on earth.

As usual, we were dumped at the basic airstrip, was right next to the main road, which was – unusually - made of Tarmac, the first bitumen I had seen since Morocco. Some nice banking at the side of the Tarmac too, good workmanship.

The camp was luxurious compared to Tichit, or the hellish Tidjeka. For a start, there were toilets and a couple of showers, set up near the base fence. When I say toilets, I think I should explain that I mean a three sided arrangement of burnt sticks and dry leaves, with an old bit of sacking for a door. You simply went inside - after paying the man who `owned' this luxury ad hoc facility of course – then squatted on a rock slab, and did what you had to do. If you wiped, got your shorts up safely and got back out without stepping on something unpleasant, then you had to consider that mission an unmitigated success.

The showers were simple black plastic bags, heated by the sun, with a trickle of water dropping into a similar leaf-built hutch. I haggled over the price for a while in the afternoon, as I was rancid after two days in a sandstorm, but the cheeky bloke running the operation was asking forty CFA, or about four quid.

I wasn't impressed and even at three quid, I passed on it. There were too many of his chums lurking near the fence too, which made me suspicious of theft. I carried my passport, money, rally pass etc. in one canvas money belt - the only time it left my fat white ass was when I showered.

I trusted nobody, I watched people closely. You had to, this was Africa and you were the prey.

The day's route to Nema was also the day's special timed stage, there were no `liaison' link sections. At some 400 kilometres, it was one of the longest too, so it was a brain-melting, body-pummelling day for the bike riders. Several bikers failed to make the final checkpoint on this stage, which was pretty much the idea from the organisers point of view.

At the front, the KTM convoy rolled on, pretty much unstoppable, with the BMWs unable to make much impression on Meoni's lead, whilst Tainan again went for the stage win, just to show how fast the KTMs could go if they felt like it. None of the leading KTMs broke down, or crashed out and I could sense that BMW felt time was running out for them.

Deaks was wrong about the KTMs breaking down, but he was right about the weather. The further South we went, the hotter it became and the afternoon sun was blistering. I sheltered inside my tent, but couldn't sleep, despite feeling utterly exhausted. I lay there in my pants, feeling sweaty, depressed and just focussing on the next meal. Not a good mental state to be in at all. There wasn't any point in filing reports anymore either, as the sand at Tidjeka had destroyed Neil's laptop.

I had been writing all my stuff on his Toshiba, then saving it to a floppy disk for satellite transfer (my Mac had no floppy drive), so I was now unable to file any reports back home for BMW. Even the BMW press team from Germany wouldn't let me use their PC laptops for half an hour a day, plus they had their own satellite phone but wouldn't entertain the idea of allowing me to send stuff to BMW GB.

Very odd isn't it? You pay 5K to send a journalist to Africa, but you won't let them use your laptop to send a report to a UK magazine. I really could not fathom what BMW were playing at, but just shrugged and went back to my tent – I really couldn't be arsed arguing with them.

All I could do was take pictures and make notes for the feature I would write back home, or at the hotel which awaited me in Dakar for three nights at the end of this madness. It wasn't even worth trying to send photos back home, as I had found out back in Atar that the TSO press office had taken a whole week to forward anything from their Paris office to the UK - anything I shot now would get home just as fast stuffed inside my rucksack.

Neil and I decided to do some pics of the riders arriving at Nema. Because the checkpoint was literally 200 metres from where our tents were pitched. The sun blazed at lunchtime as the first riders appeared, going remarkably slowly up the dirt track which petered out, just alongside the airport terminal building.

There's not a whisper of wind as the bikes thud-thud into view. The sweat pours from hair beneath my daft looking jungle hat. Later we find out from David that the cockpit temperature gauge hits 50 degrees between 2-4 p.m. I try to imagine riding across the dunes in this heat, dropping the bike, lifting 450lbs of dusty motorbike again and again, and then getting going through the soft sand washes, fighting the bike as it skews sideways.

Insane. Incredibly demoralising.

In the bivouac however, you would hardly guess that the leading riders suffer the same physical and mental energy drain that most of us flabby journalists obviously feel. The KTM pack are riding as a tight team now, following team orders, and helping Meoni along towards the finish, keeping the BMWs at bay, with Deacon and Lewis struggling to close up. Deaks, Despres and Lewis are trying their best, but finding it impossible to hack into the three hour lead that Meoni has already carved out.

I enjoy a late lunch at the bivvy, then walk the kilometre or so back to the tents. Time for some shade. I chat to a couple of people in the press tent. Most people look tired, except the French of course, who all have their secret hotel rooms booked for them at various points along the rally. They seem very cheery.

Marie-Christine, the press office boss asks around to see if there are any takers for a spare place in the press car tomorrow on the stage to Bamako in Mali. I stare at the ground and stifle a chuckle. The idea that anyone would want to spend 10 hours trapped inside a sweaty car, bouncing over sand dunes, repeatedly getting lost, has precious little appeal.

Yet now, looking back, I wish I had found the strength to try and survive that road trip, just to test every last fibre of resource, to push my luck to the very limit. Adventure is a drug that keeps flashing back to gently mock all your everyday dreams. Life now is so dull, so boringly predictable, that I would volunteer instantly.

Nema was oppressively hot, and I spent most of the day in the shade, listening to other people's stories and drinking too much beer. All I wanted to do was go home, but we still had Mali and Senegal to contend with, there was still a long way to go.

****

It was a short hop on the Fokker, maybe 30 minutes in the air, and we were free of the Sahara, gliding down into Bamako, the sprawling capital of Mali, one of the poorest countries on Earth. Something like half the country's population live in Bamako, which like all African cities has an enormous chasm between rich and poor. You could see enclaves of wealth from the air; all TV aerials, swimming pools and armed guards pacing around the perimeter roads.

We landed early in the morning and scanned the airport for a good place to make camp. There seemed to be a special section of the airport reserved for the rally planes, and a small number of troops looked back at us from behind their sunglasses

Commercial aircraft roared up and down the main runway about 600 metres away from us. There would be no daytime nap for me here.

As Neil and I pitched our tents a large smiling black man approached us, offering a handshake. Next to him was a guard with an AK47.

"Bonjour M'sieur, ca va?"
"Oui, ca va."
"Ah, you are English, American perhaps?" he asked.
"English."
"Yes, this is good. I am English too, my name is Adam-bo and I can help you today my friends. You can shower, you can have a woman if you like, perhaps a trip into the town and some beer yes?"

"Nah. I hate beer." I answered, keeping a straight face.

"That is good, good for you sir. What can I get for you then, what would you like me to do for you today?"

"Nothing, merci M'sieur." I shrugged, trying to keep an eye on Adam-bo and his mate whilst I piled stuff inside my tent quickly. Then Neil asked him how much for a shower. It was about £5, which was ridiculous. We haggled for a while, then another local guy came and argued that we on his `manor,' or whatever, but Adam-bo seemed to have a more aggressive AK47 operative in tow. The other guy left hurriedly.

"OK then, 40 Cfa for both of us, la douche froid, oui - tres, tres froid?" I insisted.
"Yes, shower is good, very cold water from a well, not far from here, forty Cfa for the big man here, and his friend."
"OK Adam-bo, I am not a big man though, I am nothing, a nobody." I joked.
"But you are here, flying around Mali on this plane, and you have money! That makes you a very big man in this place my friend." said Adam-bo.

So off we trekked, with Adam-bo and his mate, past a horde of curious, hungry faces at the airport gate and out along the service road. The further we went, the more nervous we got.

"This is bad, we could be going anywhere." said Neil.
"Not far, not far now." said Adam-bo, smiling jovially.

We walked to a checkpoint, where a huddle of soldiers stood around a small Honda moped. Talk was exchanged, possibly money too, it was hard to tell. Then we were waved past into another part of the airport compound. We trudged around a deserted concrete blockhouse. Wind moaned through broken window panes.

Finally we came to a little doorway and went inside after Adam-bo. At that moment, I half expected a clutch of Mali bandits to pop up and machete both of us to death in a whirl of butchering blows, but instead, a stale piss smell greeted us and a pair of rusting shower heads nodded at us in the gloom.

"Oh yes, showers!" said Neil.

"Good, very good yes?" enquired Adam-bo, watching us strip off our rancid desert clothes.

"Oh excellent, there's a craphouse too." I noted, looking in at the traditional hole-in-the-ground stall next to the shower. "Think I'll make a turd world donation."

We showered, Neil shaved too. We went to a private loo, without people watching us. I cannot tell you what an insanely good, life luxury that was, how exhilarating it felt. On top of those simple pleasures in life, we were not robbed, or beaten up, or raped by Adam-bo and his machine-gun toting mate.

What a bonus.

****

So feeling refreshed, we headed back to camp, and despite Adam-bo trying to double the agreed price, we felt better than we had done for several days. Water, that simple transparent thing, had infused a smile inside our souls.

We walked back past the faces of those who couldn't afford the shower, or possibly a cup of clear water, all the way to camp. The sun was rising, the heat was building up again. By the time we arrived, we smelled almost as bad as when we had set off.

"Now, you pay me extra money yes?" asked Adam-bo.
"Why?"
"I told you, shower 40 Cfa, but toilet 40 Cfa and your friend had shave - this is extra too."
"No."
"You pay me, come on, be a good man." said Adam-bo, with his AK-toting buddy getting a little closer as the action heated up.

Neil started muttering various curses - tempers soon fray in this stifling oven of a country.

"Listen Adam-bo, listen for une minute mon ami - I will buy many things from you before tomorrow my friend, so be nice to us yes?"

"We can see, yes we see." said Adam-bo, his attitude suddenly mellowing. He smiles a shark-like grin at me, and then he slapped me jovially on the shoulder;

"You are the big man here, so I will do this for you - you must wait here and I will bring girls, many girls. You will be a happy man tonight my friend."

"No girls. Just shaving, you bring me a razor eh?" I made a beard trimming gesture around my face fuzz and he smiled at me, offered a handshake at me. Instead I saluted in some bizarre gesture…more embarrassment than anything.

When Adam-bo had left, Neil shook his head in disbelief at my stupidity.
"He'll be back with a frigging circus later, you shouldn't have told him you'd buy anything."

"Well, I reckon if I bribe the guard at the gate with my porn mag, or an old T-shirt, he'll make sure Adam-bo has his airport pass taken away. If not, f**k it - what does anyone's word mean out here anyway? It's all bullshit."

****

I relaxed in my tent for an hour or so, with the porn mag so kindly donated by my colleagues at Carole Nash Insurance, and then wandered into the press tent. Today was one of the longest stages in total, at some 770 kilometres, although only about 200k of that was timed racing. The rest was `navigation,' in other words, the riders and drivers just had to survive it. No mean feat.

Another Brit journalist – let's call him Mr M - got talking to me and informed me that very few riders or vehicles were expected to arrive before 6pm today, so it would be a very quiet afternoon.

"Fancy a trip into town - there's a Sofitel here with a poolside bar service and all that jazz?"

"Yeah, why not - let's call a cab." I agreed, feeling relatively clean and presentable at that point. So we saw another Mr Fixit at the compound gate, and haggled a three quid taxi ride, which took us about five miles into town. It even included the driver actually waiting outside the hotel until we felt like returning to the rally.

Bamako is the real deal. Bamako is Africa as you imagine it would be; a riot of noise, roadside traders, stinking propane stoves, chicken blood in the gutter, cyclists sweating and an undercurrent of raw, nervous fear.

It's hard to understand real poverty in the 21st century, until you've been to somewhere like Bamako. A glimpse inside a shack, wide eyes staring back at you, or a mangy dog barking at the car. People simply cluster together in small knots of shrivelled hunger. They see your white skin and they know the truth. You are the reason they are starving, you white people are greedy, fat and you possess an enormous amount of money.

All these details build up a jigsaw in your mind, as row after row of squalid huts, pigpens, beggars pitches, offal-level food stands and a thousand other fragments of human misery unfold the cityscape beside you. We were lucky, because we just kept driving. Our battered Peugeot 504 estate taxi, which had a wooden plank upfront, instead of two regular seats, kept rattling along and I was glad we didn't break down. People would have kidnapped us within about 15 minutes.

Near the luxurious Sofitel, I saw a man with one leg sat on the roadside, his crude hut roofless, but possessing a car door as his makeshift front door. The crazy futility of his gesture made me smile. Pride is always in our nature, no matter where we stand or fall in this life.

Inside the hotel we were hit by the aircon, like a fridge in the face.

"Oh my God, that is un-fkn-believable." I said, standing still for a second and just savouring the coldness. A porter approached and asked if I was checking in, for a moment I wanted to yell, `Yes, thank Christ, give me the penthouse with the biggest bath in the world."

Instead Mr M asked the hotel manager to set us up with two sun loungers near the pool and bring us some meat-based snacks, plus the biggest, coldest beers that the Sofitel had on tap. To show that we meant business, Mr M gave the manager a discreet 10 Cfa – quite literally, his `starter for ten.'

Within about 96 seconds, all that we asked for was arranged. So we feasted on various grilled food and sank a couple of chilled lagers. The sun shone and small lizards leapt around the poolside terrace next to us. Some Russian mafia appeared and set up their camp opposite us. Two burly guys, with strangely coiffured face-fuzz and hefty bellies arrived first, sinking their bulk into their loungers. Then three, no make that four leggy, click-clacking, high-heeled women joined them, all sporting new swimming costumes, huge blingy handbags and matching sunglasses.

Two of the women sat by the pool and dangled their legs

in the water, yakking away in that aggressive, staccato Russian language that sounds both sexy and deeply sinister. I can't speak Russian but I imagine that `I love you baby' probably sounds like a death threat from a Bond villain.

Mr M seemed very taken with the Russian beauties and commented on their legs, breasts, asses, hair…the only thing he didn't seem interested in were their noses, because he rated every other part of them, in tedious detail.

"I wonder if they're aircrew, the Russians fly a load of cargo planes into Bamako so maybe they're cabin crew. We should chat `em up."
"Mate, I'm not having sex of any sort in Africa, not a chance."
"I'm not saying f*** `em over the diving board, although the blonde one looks like she'd be up for that frankly, I'm saying have a chat…buy `em a drink." soothed Mr M, who probably just wanted actual female company.

After another twenty minutes of general perving, the taller of the two girls dried her legs, put on her clacky sandals and walked around the pool. As she passed us, Mr M tried his luck;

"Hello, are you aircrew, fancy a drink?"
"What?"
"Please join us, have a few cocktails…maybe a vodka or two?"

The blonde leaned down a little closer, placing an attractive kink in her racehorse leg and looked at Mr M straight in the eye.
"F*** off."

And then off she went, with a very graceful wiggle of her cute buns. I looked at Mr M, and then glanced over at the St Petersburg heavies. One of the two mobster guys just smiled and wagged his finger at Mr M.

"Well that went well," I noted, "shall we leave now or wait for Tommy to arrive with his freakin' shine box?"

****

In any case, the afternoon unwinds nicely, with no more drama, except for an immense explosion, which echoes off the buildings. The Russians take not a jot of notice, naturally, being used to arguments being settled with guns, bombs, radioactive tea or just straightforwardly running someone over. But me and Mr M look slightly perturbed at the sound of an explosion in the vicinity. Even the lizards jumped about with extra verve just a for a second or two.

"What the hell..?"
A waiter appears to see if we need anything, I ask him what the boom was.
"Oh just a gas bottle, people use gas all the time and some people are not so good with the gas. They are smoking and cooking, so…boom-boom!"

"OK then, right."
The waiter goes off to get us one last beer apiece.

"That was never a propane bottle. That was a bomb." Says Mr M.
"Hmmm, yeah, it was pretty damn loud."
"On the upside, it sounded like it was a few miles away and there's no guns going off. So that's good."

Our third, or possibly fourth set of beers arrived and along with them, a Scandinavian bloke journalist who looked maybe 60 years old, but was probably just horribly aged by booze and cigarettes. He wore a South African style bush hat and had comedy legs sticking out of shorts that were two sizes too large. I shall call him Mr F, for legal reasons.

"Hello my friends, this is the place eh? This is the life, and this is one helluva place - mind if I join you?"

We welcomed a fellow journo of course and bought him a beer. Be rude not to. So we had a chat for an hour or so and then the sun went down. Mr M was kinda chubby and liked to eat a fair bit, so he suggested going to a decent restaurant, assuming there would a few nearby as this was the business district. In any case, the Russian ladies had gone upstairs to get changed so he had no lovely ladies to admire.

Mr F suggested we take a ride with our taxi man – who was still waiting patiently outside the front gate of the hotel – as he wouldn't charge us as much as the hotel manager. Due to the manager having taxed about 150 Cfa out of us already, on top of the beer and snack costs, we agreed.

So we put our shirts and shoes on again and paid the bill, after the usual argument about `things not included in the price.'

Our friend Mr F had no French, so it was left to myself and Mr M to explain what we wanted and haggle over the price. The taxi driver, and his `brother' eventually agreed to take us to a `top club, with steaks, music and girls, many girls.' This sealed the deal as far as Mr M was concerned, so we paid 50 Cfa each, upfront (about a fiver apiece) and got into the rickety old Peugeot again.

I sat in the front, between the driver and his brother. This was so I couldn't escape. That became apparent as we crawled through the rush hour traffic, all hooting trucks, buzzing mopeds, shouty cyclists and irate car drivers. Gradually we inched away from the wealthy area and found ourselves bumping along a dirt track, with a row of roofless shacks on one side and a gutter full of urine and offal on the other.

"Alastair, where the f*** are we going?" enquired Mr M. Good question and I really had no idea. The driver spoke some crude French phrases to me, and I tried to translate but the gist of it was simply; `steak and grand beers, many girls.'

At one point we stopped at a junction, next to a group of men huddled around a fire inside an oil drum. They looked at us inside the taxi and then laughed. This was not inspiring me with confidence at all.

"S'il vouz plait, retournez nouz dans le Sofitel, arrondissement Sofitel, allez vite."

But pleas to return to the hotel were ignored and we hit Tarmac again, for maybe two or three hundred metres, and then turned into a gateway. A huge pair of wooden gates opened and a guy with a gun waved us in.

"Oh f***, we're all gonna die." observed Mr M.
"This isn't a restaurant." said Mr F, equally observant.
I just stayed silent and smiled appreciatively at the taxi driver, as if I was delighted to be taken into this private compound. Inside I was bricking it.

Into the courtyard and then we came to a smoky halt, the diesel engine of the Peugeot having suffered a bit in the stop-start traffic. We seemed to be in the grounds of a large house, with three floors, the top floor of which was some type of nightclub. Music thumped from speakers on the terrace and it wasn't folky type yodelling, by distressed goat-herders. This was a good sign.

We got out of the taxi, beckoned on by two smartly dressed waiters in white jackets.
"You see, killers don't wear white jackets," I said casually,

"everything is gonna be fine, it's a rooftop restaurant and club. Just happens to be in the Bronx part of Bamako."

"I will wait for you, no problem M'sieur Alistair." Said the driver. Well, you could depend on that, as he opened the bonnet and began working on his wheezing vehicle with his brother helping.

The polite waiters took us upstairs, with the disco music getting louder. We reached the rooftop and saw several tables, a small pool, bar area with smiling barman, a nice BBQ grill set-up in the corner and absolutely nobody else. I mean it was a ghost town. It was like a retirement party for Vladimir Putin in Kiev.

There was nothing else to do but sit down and order a drink.
"Le petit beer, or trois grande beer?" enquired a suave, white jacketed waiter.
"Er, trois grande beers, s'il vouz plait."

When they arrived we all looked at each other and laughed. The bottles were huuuge, must have had at least one litre of lager inside them and on the label it read; `Grand Beer.' Yep, does what it says on the bottle my friends. I will drink to no-nonsense Mali brewers.

We ordered a steak each, having debated the prices with the fervour of angry students at Oxford University, who had accidentally bumped into Northerners at a dinner party. Just then the disco music stopped and a small posse of drummers appeared.

"What the...we are not paying for this, non cadeaux, non!" said Mr M, who was wise to ways of the locals. But then his mood softened, as a troupe of young female dancers came bounding up the steps, wearing slash-cut dresses that showed off their athletic legs nicely. Even Mr F was getting frisky, and he probably hadn't had an erection since the early 1990s.

The dancers put on a marvellous show, with the general flavour being Beyoncé meets the cheerleaders from the L.A. Lakers. It was slightly difficult to eat steak with any shred of dignity, whilst a young lady jiggled her cleavage next to you, but somehow I managed. Fear does sometimes spark an appetite.

The dancers stopped for a break and their drummers/minders then hassled us for about £100, which was obviously ludicrous. We ate, drank our beers the size of wine bottles, and merrily haggled the down to £30 or so. Then they asked us which girls we liked best…uh-oh.

Both Mr F and M were tempted, maybe the drinking had given them Dutch courage, but I was adamant that we were leaving. I felt sure we'd be robbed off everything, possibly worse. We were miles out of town and these guys could make us dig our own graves and murder us before any Police would arrive.

"Right, we have to be nice, really nice. We have to go back to the airport, because this isn't a club, it's a knocking shop and we're going to be taxed of all our cash anyway. So I say, let's smile, get the taxi fare together and give the rest of our money to these nice ladies – then leave."

Mr M wasn't happy about this arrangement, mainly because he had the most cash out of the three of us. But he also felt he should `get something, just see some tits or something,' for the donation.

"Well, being alive tomorrow is good – what's that worth?" I asked, before we divvied up our money and handed it over.

In total, that meal out of town – way, way out of town – probably cost the three of us about £60 each. But when you consider the following, you can see the real value:

1. Not getting killed
2. Not getting HIV/Aids
3. Eating actual cow steak, not dog

Result: Priceless.

****

The journey home seemed to take an age, as our driver constantly badgered me for more money, convinced I was hiding some cash on my person. I wasn't but I did give him a Carole Nash Insurance pen, which in many ways is worth more than 10 Cfa. Collector's item mate. One of only 25,000 ever made, that year.

We had to stop in a dubious area and all three of us took an immense leak, as the effects of the Grande Beer kicked in. It was incredibly nerve-wracking watching locals moving slowly nearer to us as we added to the open sewer problems of Mali. But we got back on the move and boy was I glad to see the armed guards at the airport gate waving at the Peugeot to stop, well short of the barrier.

Mr F and Mr M walked inside, fed up at being bilked for all their cash, whilst I placated both the guards and the taxi man, both of whom saw one more chance for cash. I turned out my pockets and shrugged like a Frenchman, wished everyone a beery `Bon nuit' and staggered into the camp.

My photo buddy Neil was in the press tent, writing up some news on a friend's laptop.

"Big night out in Bamako then?"

"Oh yeah, dancing girls, steaks the size of your head and beers like skittles. Might buy a second home here."

"You're really pissed mate. Funny."

"Pissed, broke and alive, it doesn't get any better on the Dakar Neil."

Actually, I wasn't broke, as I hadn't thought it wise to take all my cash into Bamako, so I'd hidden about £200 in Cfa inside some old camera film canisters. Remember those little plastic boxes? Fortunately, nobody had nicked my rucksack, which was still inside Neil's tent.

I was glad I'd seen Bamako, but equally glad that we were leaving in the morning. Mali remains the poorest place on earth that I've ever seen and the desperation is so heavy in the air, you can taste it. It permeates your very soul and steals away your humanity by the hour.

In the end, all you want to do is leave the stinking, mosquito-infested, lizard-leaping hell-hole as soon as you can, which is probably how most of the locals feel too.

****

CHAPTER SEVEN:

THE GREEN, GREEN, GRASS OF HOME

What can I tell you about Bakel?

Not much, as I stayed away from the town itself, which is perhaps 5 or 10Kms away from the airport. Bakel is another one of those old French Foreign Legion outposts, with the ruins of a fort, set on a hill overlooking a river. The TSO press office staff made it sound interesting, but by this stage of the rally I was too mentally and physically exhausted to bother sight-seeing.

We arrived quite late in the day and it was nice to see some greenery, lots of trees, after the bleakness of the terrain around Bamako airport. I was heartily sick of airports and sleeping on gravel and Tarmac.

There was already a kind of camp set up at one end of the runway, not far from a busy main road – a Tarmac road too. Lots of local Senegalese men came buzzing past on scooters and bicycles, shouting at us to buy things, or just give them money. We were fenced off, but they could have easily broken through. The big difference was that Senegal was obviously quite wealthy compared to Mali, so you felt a bit safer.

I pitched the tent and slept for a while, then near sunset I made my way to the bivvy for some food. The stage was a long one for the riders and some arrived at the bivouac as I ate and drank a beer or two. Per Lundmark, a KTM privateer had a ripe, painful bruise on his face, the result of being pitched over the handlebars a couple of days previously. Other riders bled when they took off their gloves, their hands cracked and tender.

Deaks was still hammering the big BMW and had made up some more precious minutes on the lead group of KTMs, but Meoni was about 3 hours in front. Unless Meoni, Arcarons, Pujol, Cox, and De Garvado all crashed out, it looked like a KTM `clean sweep' on the podium.

The mood in the BMW camp was pretty downbeat all round. Everyone, BMW head office included, had expected more from the team. The plan had been for Roma to win, Despres and Deacon to get 3rd and 4th place maybe, Jimmy Lewis in 6th. But in my view, the 900cc bike was a liability on a rally raid like this; top heavy, too thirsty on fuel and difficult for the average rider to drag out of a sand wash.

John Deacon was arguably the only rider in the team capable of manhandling this great lummox of a motorcycle upright five or six times an hour, without risking passing out. Considering this was a German team, nobody seemed to have thought of that brutal reality – riders fall off quite often riding in soft sand. When they bin it, they alone have to pick the bugger up in sweltering heat and that is a job for a big, burly bloke.

The thing about the Dakar is that it's a race where the rider matters more than the machine. Especially the psychological toughness of the rider. Coping with the organiser's constant chicanery, rule-bending, lying and French bias is difficult. Then you have the route itself through the Western Sahara; strength-sapping, full of danger and it's a very lonely event. Mercilessly lonely, compared to almost every other type of motorsport.

No pit lane radio, no signals telling you how your rivals are doing, and no human contact if you get lost. There's just you and every inner resource you can muster – it truly is like war without the bullets.

For me, this was the weakness within BMW's team. They lacked an appreciation of the mental scale of the challenge and how much psychological support riders needed. There was no team spirit in the BMW camp, which is a vital ingredient. I saw this poor planning again when TV adventure biker Charley Boorman signed up for the event, a few years later.

I went to the London press conference where Charley was kitted up in full BMW biking regalia, with buddy Ewan McGregor (yeah that film actor fella) there for moral support. A bespoke rally racing 650 enduro bike, all ready to ride, was there for Charley. PR agency people milled around, sponsors were schmoozing too – it was an expensive jaunt, with a TV show in place as well. There was an intro, then a question and answer session. I put my hand up immediately and asked;

"What sort of mental preparation have you made to deal with the psychological toughness of the race Charley?"

"Wanking mainly. Next question."

Oh how the room laughed, as Charley put down the old journo with his witty one-liner. But I bet nobody from BMW was laughing when Charley crashed in Morocco, a mere three days into the event, breaking both wrists because he woefully underestimated how mentally tough it is to ride over rocks for 10 hours.

That was the effective end of the TV series built around the `Charley Does the Dakar' concept – frankly a ton of money was spent on a not-very-interesting travelogue, presented by an amiable bloke with two plaster casts on his wrists, instead of watching a professional bike racer winning the Everest of off-road racing, which would have been much more interesting, some might say.

Yes, the Dakar is like climbing the Everest, or tackling the Isle of Man TT races. It requires dedication, a Zen-like approach to learning every inch of the route, and the internal politics which underpin the event. It's a vocation, not a race. Years of preparation, not just a few months, are advisable.

The great riders of the TT races; Joey Dunlop, Dave Jefferies and John McGuinness, all spent years acquiring a craftsmanship, a subtle suit of psychological armour if you like, to cope with its cobra-like dangers. One error, one lapse of concentration and…that's it, you're gone.

****

I couldn't cope with being a hanger-on journo on the Dakar, never mind ride a motorcycle that far. My mental state was worsening by the day in that fierce heat. In truth, by the time I lay in a tent in Bakel, my mind was crumbling and I just wanted out of this crazy circus.

To liven up the press tent noticeboard, I cut pages out of my porn mag and pasted them next to the race reports. Not just photos of women showing their flange either, but random words and phrases like `come all over my butt' etc. which I glued onto dull rally reports in a Joe Orton style act of sabotage.

Amazingly, many people didn't even blink as they read the latest on who was in 48th place, at the second waypoint, whilst being `shafted rotten by husband's best mate' that day.

I almost collapsed laughing as the Japanese journo, who wore immaculate white gloves, pursed his lips, in a mild disgust, as he scanned the noticeboard. Then he walked around the other side of it, checked the porn there too, frowned, and then casually went back to the first side.

Later that night, I woke up, needing a beer-fuelled pee in the ditch nearby. Lizards scattered in the glow from my head torch. The generators thrummed away by the press planes, French and Spanish voices laughed and chattered, some 150 metres from me. I had given them the gift of late night porn, and all was well in the world.

Suddenly there was a sharp crackling in the distance, then a heavier 'crump' kinda noise. Voices fell silent. There was a momentary silence, then a rapid exchange of fire, somewhere near the border with Mali, which was perhaps 10 or 15 kilometres away. It could've been slavers or drug dealers, settling differences, or Islamist rebels exacting revenge on someone. Or perhaps border security guards getting twitchy and firing at shadows.

The noise paused as I stopped peeing mid-flow, but then it crackled into life again when I had finished. It didn't get louder, in fact it rattled away more distantly, so that was OK. Like thunder, it faded across the sky. I went back to sleep thinking that if we were robbed, then that was OK with me. Just take it, take it all. This is your home, your domain, not mine.

****

Next morning, several journos asked me about the mysterious porno updates on the bulletin board and the TSO staff seemed a bit frosty. Oh well, what goes on the tour and all that. I just shrugged and asked what time we were leaving Bakel.

We packed again and took an early flight for Tambacounda, the last stop before Dakar itself. On the plane, I sat next to a Senegalese journalist, who had been covering the race for the first time, like me, and had mixed feelings about the event. We chatted for the duration of the flight, as he opened up gradually to me, trusting me with his real opinions.

"We are proud that someone from Senegal is competing, but this often feels like a French race, not an international race. It's like there are two classes of teams and drivers. In football, players from Senegal can go and play anywhere, they don't have to join a French team. But on the Dakar, if you aren't in a French team, with French money, then…mmm, who knows?"

I agreed with him and went further;

"All this stuff with Schlesser and his Renault buggies, the media frenzy around him, says it all. They want French drivers, riders and teams to win the event if possible. Richard Sainct would never get a time penalty for pushing his BMW backwards, but John Deacon does – le rosbif. The race is like a little French Foreign Legion picnic, an old school reunion. That's what it feels like to me."

He smiled, looked out of the window of the Fokker.

"My family are down there waiting for me. They think I'm an important man now because I am on this plane. But it's not like that. The really important men are people like you, because you can tell the world what it's really like – I cannot speak. I dare not write the truth."

I nodded in agreement and tried to imagine what it must be like to work in a country where the `party line' has to be adhered to, strictly, or else you face poverty, or worse.

The heat was intense when we landed and it was probably only 9am or so. There was a small airport building, a little fence and a gatehouse; most of the remaining journos were camping near the buildings.

Some other journalists, as well as my friend from Senegal, had baled out on this stop and just gone straight to Dakar by road. The capital of Senegal was a major city, with hotels, air con, beers, swimming pools, taxis, TV – unlike Tambacounda, which was a provincial backwater. In some respects, the race was all but over, certainly in the bikes class. But I thought I'd stick to the route, just in case there was some last minute upset on the race, some drama.

There wasn't in the motorcycle class, where Cyril Despres took the stage win but John Deacon stayed in touch to hang onto 6th place overall. However in the cars section, Schlesser was getting increasingly ragged as he battled with the Mitsubishis of Kleinschmidt and Matsuoka. It was anyone's race when they rolled into Tambacounda, with just one big mileage stage left.

You could sense the tension in the pits late that afternoon and I spent time walking about in the cars section of the paddock, chatting and taking pictures.

The Renault buggies driven by Servia and Schlesser were the coolest looking vehicles in the event, but I disliked Schlesser intensely. He had that typical racer arrogance, full of self-regard and a conviction that he had a divine right to win. Schlesser ignored people who were no use to him and drove like a crazy man. You felt that someone would get killed or hurt if he didn't win.

As I slept that night, big red ants marched into my tent, attracted by the sugary snacks I had stashed in there no doubt, and I awoke about 4 am, as a line of ants – each one about 3mm long - chomped down on my tasty white flesh. I felt the pain obviously, which woke me from my exhaustion, then I switched on my torch and looked inside my sleeping bag. Yep, there they were – a mass of crawling buggers, all busily biting my leg. There were dozens in a line, marching up towards my knees.

As I started swearing and tried to move my tent, I suddenly saw that I had pitched my tent right on top of their nest. Oh brilliant. The ruckus also annoyed the ants who really began to move fast, as I tried to relocate my tent about 20 metres away. I left the sugar cereal bar near their nest – distraction ploy worked, eventually.

It took about an hour to de-ant my clothing and tent, pitch it next to a track, which seemed insect-free, and apply some suntan lotion to the wounds. Probably did about as much good as rubbing dock leaves on nettle stings, but you have to work with the tools available.

I was bleary eyed the next day and grumpy, with evil red bumps and bleeding lumps on my legs. Someone took pity on me and sent me to the medical tent, where they cleaned things up properly and put a huge plaster over the worst cluster of bites. That felt damn good. I said `merci' and meant it. Not every French person is a swine y'know.

The start of the final dash to Dakar was dramatic as Servia and Schlesser jumped the queue, getting ahead of the Mitsubishi 4X4s. Matsuoka broke his suspension taking the scenic route off-piste around Schlesser, so that seemed to be race over. But the crafty Dakar officials had an ace up their sleeve – yes, the old `time penalty ploy M'sieur!'

So Schlesser got stuffed with a 90 minute or so penalty, and as Jutta Kleinschmidt had spent the day banging her Mitsubishi right up Schlesser's arse, she was now in the lead overall. The cars section was going right down to the wire, with the last stage around the pink lake (the Lac Rose) being the decider after 10,000kms. Wow.

The bikes section was all over bar the shouting and Meoni was still three hours ahead, so he could thrap around the lake in 5th gear, singing 'When the moon hits your eye, like a big pizza pie, that's Amore...' and still win.

For me, the adventure was over too. We touched down at Dakar airport and I forgot my Mac computer, still abandoned in the Fokker's overhead locker since Morocco. Luckily the Danish aircrew did a final sweep of the plane before we left. They passed the laptop to me and offered a cheery farewell. I said 'thank you' in a monotone and just sat on the runway, touching the Tarmac with my fingers.

Neil looked at me; bedraggled, sunburnt, hung over and driven half crazy by Lariam, sleep deprivation. My legs were well bitten by angry insects.

"Are you OK, do you need a doctor or anything?"

It was only then that I realised how ill I must have looked. How utterly drained. But that's what three weeks of sleeping rough, fighting sandstorms, arguing over chairs in bivouacs, scary plane landings, lack of sleep and too much alcohol can do.

"It's OK Neil, I have a hotel booked. Two nights, clean sheets, aircon, beers in the fridge. I shall see you tomorrow after the Lac Rose stage buddy."

So I jumped in a taxi and we drove through the streets of Dakar. The colours exploded from the pavement into my eyes; trees, people in yellow, green, red, shouting children, beeping cars and scooters, chickens in the roads. A riot of civilisation set next door to a blue, supermarine blue ocean. The haze of salt and heat, shimmering in your eyes.

Like a crazed spaniel, I draped my head out of the yellow

taxi window and tasted the sea air. Smelled the food cooking at the roadside, inhaled the two stroke oil from the battered Peugeot scooters. Being in Dakar, was like emerging from a three week coma, it was life amplified. Full noise.

"Better than desert yes?" asked my taxi man.
"Hell yes. The desert is nothing at first, and then it makes you like nothing. A speck of dust."

"Yes, desert very bad, bad for dust. You want beers? We can get ice cold beers, I know a good place."

I smiled at his cheeky ploy. This was still Africa; everyone was on the make, all the time, relentless as wheels going around. Chasing circles in the sand.

"No mon ami, just le hotel, s'il vouz plait."

****

Bonjour M'sieur, checking in?"

God yes, checking in.

Checking in this stinking tent and rancid sleeping bag – which I heartily donate to the porter, who shows me to my room. Yes, I'm also checking in my socks and underpants, which I throw in the bin as soon as I strip off. Then finally, blissfully, I am shedding the last specks of desert, the grains of Sahara imbued within my skin, as I shower for what seems like an hour. Sweet, warm water, and rich, slippery soap. Oh how I have missed your humanising touch.

Afterwards, wrapped in a towel, I walk onto the balcony of my room and look down some 12 floors or so. People sit around the pool sipping drinks, and armed guards wander in the streets nearby. Traffic toots and lurches past.

Everything is normal. Boys play football on the beach and shout the same nonsense that boys everywhere do.

I go back inside and lie on the soft, springy bed. It feels strange, ridiculously decadent and comfortable. I can't quite sleep, even though I feel worn out and scrubbed clean now. I miss the aircraft noise, the quad bikes rushing by to the bivouac, the babel of languages in the tented area near the planes. This room, with its sterile desk and plastic phone is weird, almost claustrophobic, and prison-like.

I doze for a few hours in the afternoon after ordering a hamburger from room service, and ice cold beer. Then I try watching TV for a while but it bores me. I take some photos from the balcony and then get dressed. I decide to visit the Meridian hotel, which is way, way across town. This is where the rally HQ is located. I want to know who won the race, I'll never sleep if I don't find out. So I go outside to haggle over a taxi, refusing the bell boy's kind offer of assistance.

It only takes a few minutes to negotiate a fair price. I'm an old hand at haggling now after three weeks in Africa, recognising the fake smiles, the little dabs of fingertip to nose, or glances aside, that betray a lie. I can see desperation in a man's eyes, just as he can see through my sunglasses into my scaredy-cat, white man weaknesses.

We shake hands on a price, return journey included, because I don't care to bargain all over again at the Meridian, where the price will be super extortionate, as this is the `official' Dakar hotel. Room rates are about £220 a night, which for Senegal is ridiculous, even in January. So I'm not paying tourist taxi rates back.

I climb into the front of the Renault and sit alongside my driver, because I hate sitting in the back. It's like you're setting up a British class system straight away and I despise business people who sit in the back of taxis, wittering away on their phones. Making themselves immune from what's around them.

The traffic is crazy, so progress is slow but I like that, as I hang out of the window and let the camcorder film a few minutes of fried chicken stands, music pumping from café speakers, kids running alongside the cab. We reach the main coast road and the buildings thin out a bit, vacant areas feature mangy animals and people sitting in the shade, looking utterly defeated, lost. Poverty always wears the same crumpled blanket face, in every corner of the world.

Suddenly we screech to a halt. A black Range Rover, with blacked out windows heads towards us at speed, hogging the middle of the road.

"It is the President, the President is passing by. We must stop and wave." says my driver. Another 4X4, which could have been a Ford Bronco or something hurtles past and then we can see the stretch limo, complete with little flags fluttering on the wings. My driver smiles and waves. I just stare.

There's a cloud of dust and heat as the limo swooshes by, but we can't see inside of course. It could have been the President's mistress off to get her hair done for all we know. A rear-guard 4X4 then goes past, with four soldiers sat in the back of the Ford Ranger pick-up.

"Now you must be a lucky man my friend," says my driver, "it's a good omen to see the President, it brings us blessings."

"Really?"
"Yes really."

I look across the road at a man sat in the doorway of a burnt out school bus. You can see a few flecks of yellow paint near the back of it, mixed in with twisted, half melted metal and brown ocean sprayed rust. It sits on two huge lumps of concrete, like some surrealist static caravan. The man is smoking. Even though he has nothing, he smokes. That's the way it is.

I guess if you live in a shell of a bus, with no shoes, no job and you get to watch the President's motorcade go by, then cancer might be a blessing. I don't know.

****

So when I reach the Meridian, and everyone is taking photos of each other, swapping emails and promising to keep in touch, I'm in a strange mood. This obscene luxury is so alien, yet so familiar and it's like a switch has been flicked. Journalists who didn't speak three words to me in three weeks, are now my bosom buddies for life because, apparently, `we shared the adventure, and we made it to Dakar.'

What a load of bollocks. TSO got us to Dakar. I ask one journo how he liked the hotels in Atar, Bamako and Tambacounda, were they comfortable? Adventure my arse.

I bump into Meoni, as he gets more photos done and signs people's programmes, press kits, T-shirts etc. He is beaming with unvarnished delight at winning the Dakar and looks like a gladiator after a famous victory, all sweat, tears and burnished skin. Fabrizio is similar to John Deacon, both have the build of farmer's sons, hewn from the iron earth.

Mconi's wife and son have flown out to meet him, so there's a huge amount of emotion in the terrace bars at the Meridian, after today's Lac Rose stage. Jutta Kleinschmidt has won the cars section too – the first woman to ever win a

Dakar. She too keeps breaking down in tears.

The daylight fades and after a few beers, I decide to head back to my hotel. I say goodbye to Neil, my photo buddy, who promises to send a batch of slides to my office as soon as he can. This he does. I miss Alberto, maybe he left, or maybe he went drinking with Meoni, who knows?

My driver is still waiting at the end of the hotel drive. They won't let him in of course, as he isn't on the local kickback system with the Concierge. But off we go into the night, a faster trip this time and I take some more film on the camcorder before he advises me to keep my head – and camera – inside the window.

In my room later, I finally sleep, having packed my rucksack for the trip home. It must be about 10 pounds lighter now, I've given so much away. Plus the tent and sleeping bag are gone too, donated to a hotel porter, so it will be easy at the airport. Then I slide into oblivion and don't wake up for about ten hours.

The race is run.

****

EPILOGUE: ROMAN HOLIDAY

It was spring 2006 when I finally got to Rome, taking a long weekend there with my then girlfriend. We did the usual tourist things; the Coliseum, the Trevi Fountains, you know how it goes. But as we walked around the busy streets, I turned a corner and saw a sign saying `Moto Show Roma' or something similar.

"I didn't even know this was on, let's take a look."

"Yeah right." said my girlfriend, but fair play she wandered inside the show halls, which were quite small really, a bit like a rural Town Hall might be in the USA or UK. Then I walked through a little archway and saw a huge photo of the recently deceased Fabrizio Meoni on the wall. There was his Dakar winning KTM too, the one I remembered from the race. Covered in dirt, sand and dust from the last rally.

I stood still by the bike for a second or two and then touched it. I had never dared touch it on the race itself. Somehow I wanted to connect with the Dakar race that I had been on, just by reaching out to that winning bike, the one I'd seen on the podium at the Meridian, near the Lac Rose. Memories filled my head.

The stand had lots of photos of Meoni, his achievements in bike racing and was a tribute to a fallen hero, as Fabrizio had died in the 2005 Dakar race.

My girlfriend could see I'd gone quiet and asked me if I knew him, so I explained about the race, how tough it was and how Fabrizio's young son had stood next to him on the winner's step in Senegal. There were a couple of guys working on the stand and although they didn't speak much English, and my Italian is non-existent, I managed to explain that I'd met Meoni and written a feature on the 2001 edition of the race.

Great guys that they were, they insisted on having a photo taken with me stood next to the bike. Shook my hand, thanked me for sharing memories.

I used their computer and showed them the feature I'd written about the Dakar, in a kind of desert journal style. They humoured me and pretended to be impressed, but anyway, it meant a great deal to me at the time. Just saying that I knew Meoni, saw how hard he fought for that win, added something to their day, and mine.

By then, John Deacon had also died, falling from his bike in Syria in another off-road race. Nobody really knew why he died, his injuries were fairly slight, it just seemed his heart had given out, right there in the desert. Even giants fall someday, their energy banks running suddenly dry. Fragments of my motorcycling past were already dust, nothing more than memories, within a few short years.

It felt odd inside that motorcycle show, being back in the Sahara, listening to the incessant roar of the Hercules, the drone of quad bikes heading to the bivouac, the shouts of `Cadeaux, cadeaux!' Just for a few minutes I felt it come alive again, in the heat of the Italian sun.

The race itself moved to South America a few years after Meoni's death, beaten by terror threats and a slow disintegration into civil war within Mali, which made that country too dangerous to visit. It's a safer race, but a very different event now, having been airlifted to a different continent.

In the end, the desert will cover all our tracks, but I like to think that underneath those dunes archaeologists will one day discover tent pegs from Millets camping stores, a random T-shirt, still imbued with John Deacon's sweat, or a wrapper from an energy bar, consumed by Fabrizio just before he fell asleep, exhausted after another stage win.

Maybe they will piece together the jigsaw of the Dakar from all those clues, those grains of truth, and marvel.

As I did.

The End

ABOUT THE AUTHOR

Alastair Walker has freelanced for dozens of motorcycle and car magazines and written over 2000 features. He was the founding editor of insidebikes.com, one of the first internet motorcycle magazines.

He wrote *The Café Racer Phenomenon* and a history of Kawasaki two stroke triples for Veloce Books UK, plus *Scooterama* for Carlton Books.

Jacks, Knaves and Kings of Speed, a series of brief biographies is available on Kindle, plus *Notes From The Margins*, a series of essays on contemporary politics and culture.

Printed in Great Britain
by Amazon